Journey To The Top Of Africa

Crossing the Amboselli,
Climbing Mt. Kilimanjaro &
Exploring the Ngorongoro Crater

Patrick Mages

St. Brendan Press

www.journeytothetopofafrica.com

T0368202

Copyright © 2006 by Patrick Mages.

Library of Congress Control Number: 2005908719

ISBN 10:   Hardcover   1-59926-840-X
                      Softcover   1-59926-839-6

ISBN 13:   Hardcover   978-1-59926-840-8
                      Softcover   978-1-59926-839-2

All rights reserved. No part of this book may be reproduced or transmitted in any form or by any means, electronic or mechanical, including photocopying, recording, or by any information storage and retrieval system, without permission in writing from the copyright owner.

This book was printed in the United States of America.

To order additional copies of this book, contact:

Xlibris Corporation

1-888-795-4274

www.Xlibris.com

Orders@Xlibris.com

29834

For James M. "Jim" Carman, PhD.
The finest man I have ever known.

"Once a journey is designed, equipped, and put into process, a new factor enters and takes over. A trip, a safari, an exploration, is an entity, different from all other journeys. It has personality, temperament, individuality, uniqueness. A journey is a person in itself; no two are alike. And all the plans, safeguards, policing, and coercion are fruitless. We find after years of struggle that **we do not take a trip, a trip takes us.**"

John Steinbeck
Travels With Charley

CONTENTS

"Which Hospital Are You From, Lad?"

Mt. Ben Nevis can be mean as an angry snake and I really do not like snakes. Ben Nevis, in the western highlands of Scotland, is not high as mountains go. It is but 4,406 feet, much short of a mile high. In some countries it would be called a hill or a minor inconvenience.

I elected to do a solo climb of Ben Nevis in May of 1986 as part of a steep and self inflicted mountaineering learning curve. Mountains had entered my psyche and my soul in the Colorado Rockies a few years earlier. I had struggled up my very first high mountain near Aspen and, once at the summit looking down on other mountains, I was hooked forever. That day I made a personal commitment to climb mountains throughout the world.

While studying the high points of the United Kingdom and Ireland I discovered that British Everest teams and British Special Forces had trained on Mt. Ben Nevis. The Ben seemed like a proper step in my mountaineering education, my quest to go higher and higher. It was also one I felt I could do alone.

The weather in northwestern Scotland was wet, wetter, wettest. I found the portal to Ben Nevis just outside the lovely little town of Fort William and, on two successive days, climbed a few hundred feet only to realize the mountain was spitting everything it had in my direction. Footing was abysmal, visibility was marginal, and I was decidedly not duck-like in any way. On both days I retreated to the relative warmth of the Craig Dhu, on Loch Linneh, just south of Fort William.

The Craig Dhu, or Black Rock, served as my base camp. I soon discovered I had a flair for picking comfortable base camps. The Craig, once the ancestral home of the McPherson clan, was now a comfortable hotel operated by the Hanson family. I selected a room in the old mansion and rode out the weather in the proper dining room and in the miniature pub behind the reception desk. Each day I would don my Gore-Tex, shoulder my pack and head for Ben Nevis. And each day I would drive back to the Craig, strip off wet clothing, brew a cup of tea, enjoy a hot shower, dress for dinner and promise myself the weather gods of The Ben would be kinder on the morrow.

I was once diagnosed as an incurable optimist. No antidote available. Then came the diagnosis as an incurable romantic. No antidote possible. The third diagnosis: masochist, which explained my interest in mountaineering.

On the third day the weather was so perfectly terrible I decided to pack my things, leave base camp (The Craig) and drive to the Isle of Skye for a look at the Black Cullens, a series of fabled peaks. At the village of Kyle-Of-Lochlash I crossed to the island on a ferry and watched the ever-present rain and mist envelop the mountains.

There is a persistent rumor that once upon a time and very, verrrry long ago, a strange warm and yellow light had been seen in the sky above Scotland, but I couldn't confirm it.

I motored up the eastern coast of Skye to the city of Portree, which boasted a harbor so perfect it seemed as if Hollywood had created a set for some tartan plaid motion picture. The hotel above the harbor had plenty of rooms, a bar with scotch whiskey and a kitchen with perfect cold smoked Scottish salmon. I am, I decided, a base camp bon vivant.

The hotel bar was quiet. Two local lads and a barman were talking football (soccer), the national religion. I politely inquired if there was a local scotch I might try. The barman, hearing my American voice, asked which state I was from and expressed surprise that I would choose to vacation at this time of year. "Bit wet now, ya know." I knew.

He ran down some of the scotch on hand and I paused attempting to make a decision. One of the local lads then interceded. "Aye, Sean, give him some of the good stuff, he's come a long way." Sean looked at the local lad as if to say, "Really, share the good stuff with 'em?" "Give 'em a taste of the good stuff, you wanker," said the other lad. Wanker, I later learned, is not a term of endearment. Sean shrugged, reached beneath the bar and produced a mason jar with a screw type cap. The crude label indicated it was "Olde Pig Stye" and obviously very local.

Sean poured two fingers of scotch into a glass. I was tempted to ask for an ice cube or two, normal in the States, but here it would have been a transgression of huge proportion. I decided I was in Rome and lifted the glass. I checked the color, which was unremarkable, nosed the scotch, (it was scotch whiskey) and took a sip. The barman and the two lads watched with interest. The pressure was on for this was private stock and "some of the good stuff."

I rolled it on my tongue. My tongue protested. It was, without any question, the worst scotch I had ever tasted. I tried a second hit. No improvement. The lads watched with keen interest.

I weighed my options. I could be polite and offer a compliment in the face of their generosity to the traveler far from home. Or I could tell the truth.

"Gentlemen, no offense please, but this is the worst scotch I have ever tasted."

They erupted and pounded the bar, then advanced on me, shook my hand and pounded my back, laughing all the way. When the laughter finally subsided, Sean drew himself together, found a clean glass and poured two fingers of Lagavulin, on the house. Lagavulin proved to be heavenly.

It seems that when the dregs of a bottle did not constitute a full serving they would pour it into the "Old Pig Stye" jar. There must have been dozens of different dregs of scotch in the jar. They then pass the ghastly mixture off on unsuspecting tourists as a practical joke. I had not taken the bait and they loved it.

"Ah, lad there was a German who insisted it was mother's milk and wanted to know where he could buy a case."

"There was the Japanese who wanted to meet the distiller. Totally full of shite, he was."

Both of the local lads had served in Her Majesty's forces and they were still unhappy with anything German or Japanese. So, they viewed a shot of Old Pig Stye as a true chemical weapon.

Apparently I passed their test for we became friendly and they even apologized, which, I explained, isn't necessary when you are allies.

Since the weather on the Isle of Skye was no better, and sometimes marginally worse than Fort William, I spent the night in Portree and returned to the Craig Dhu, where I was greeted by Martha, a lovely raven haired beauty who held most of the jobs at the Inn, including receptionist, chamber maid, room service waitress and publican (she presided over the pub when the elder Hanson's retired for the night).

"So, you're back for another try at it," said Martha.

"Yes, I'm determined and tomorrow is the day, since I must leave for home the day after," I replied.

"Well, dinner is at six, so clean up and make yourself presentable. It's venison tonight and if I were you I wouldn't miss it. You're sure to need your strength for The Ben."

"Have you any scotch on hand in your petite pub?" I'm a master at the dumb question, but I wanted to see the expression on her face.

"Are ya daft?" And she put her head back and laughed. "Ah, Patrick, we call it 'whiskey' and sure, we have a lot unless I beat you to it. I don't mind a dram or two later on."

"But do you have the best? For example do you have Lagavulin?"

"Yes, sure and about a dozen others. We have the best."

"Ah, then you would have Old Pig Stye, no doubt."

"Sorry, Old what?"

"Old Pig Stye. You must, it's a classic."

"Well, we have plenty of male pigs who come into the pub, but no whiskey by that name."

"A shame, it is memorable."

Mr. Hanson was in jacket and tie. Mrs. Hanson greeted me at the door wearing white gloves. Dinner at six. Wonderful roast venison. And then to the pub. Martha, in her role as publican and quality control chief, matched me shot for shot. Then at ten she rang the bell and announced that by order of village law the pub must close. I began to leave when a local farmer in bib overalls grabbed my arm and said, "Sit, lad." Like a faithful dog, I complied for he was a very strong farmer.

Martha turned the lights out, left the bar and locked the front door of the Inn. Ten of us, one American and nine locals, sat in the dark. Martha returned. The lights came on and she announced, "The Hanson private family bar is now open." And scotch was once again poured. What a great country.

Paddy, the farmer, and I exchanged jokes much to the delight of the locals. I did my best to keep up, but clearly he was a superior storehouse of humor. The category was bankers.

I offered this one: "When dealing with a banker who has a glass eye, any warmth of human kindness will appear in the glass eye." The crowd roared approval. And then Paddy wheeled out his heavy guns.

"Well, Patrick, that's a good one, sure. But have you heard about farmer McTavish who went into Fort William each year for his annual loan. He asked for banker McDougal. He and McDougal had been negotiating for years and McTavish always lost. A young clerk told McTavish that banker McDougal had died that very day."

"He died," said farmer McTavish?"

"Yes sir, died," confirmed the clerk

The next day the farmer returned to the bank and again asked for banker McDougal. And again the young clerk explained that banker McDougal had died two days ago. The farmer left.

The third day the farmer returned to the bank and once again asked for banker McDougal. The young clerk looked at the farmer and said, "Sir, banker McDougal died three days ago. And

I told you that the first day, again the second day and now I'm telling you once more, banker McDougal is dead. Do you understand, he's dead, so why are you asking me again?"

"Sorry lad, but I so love hearing it."

I convulsed. The locals hammered the table with hands and glasses. Martha roared. And Paddy, the farmer beamed and chuckled at his own Scottish humor. He won. It was no contest. Scot humor at its finest. I laughed so hard I spilled my scotch. Martha replaced it and dabbed a damp towel on my last clean shirt.

We shared a final toast, everyone wished me well on the Ben Nevis climb and Martha gave me a kiss on the cheek for good luck.

I arrived in Fort William early in the morning and found an excellent outdoor shop appropriately named Nevisport. I purchased an ice axe since I had learned there was some slippery ice and snow near the summit this time of year.

As I was browsing the shop I wandered into the map section. I had always heard that British cartographers were among the best, and the maps I opened were better than any I had ever seen. If a farm, for example, had a small out building it would be on the map. I pursued maps of the area and then thumbed a map that aroused my curiosity—Mt. Kilimanjaro. It was actually a map of southern Kenya and northern Tanzania. And there was the highest mountain in Africa, the fabled Kilimanjaro. I purchased the map and tucked it into my pack. I'm one of the few to climb Mt. Ben Nevis in a blinding blizzard with a map of East Africa as reading material. Mad dogs and Englishmen . . . and Americans. Indeed.

My solo climb of Ben Nevis was a study in weather. Mist at the base, light rain at 1000 feet, hail and slush at 2000 feet, patches of snow and exposed rock and skree (small broken rock) at 3000 feet and a blizzard at the summit.

Half way up the mountain I encountered a rushing stream that had cut a deep channel through the snow and ice field. Climbing down into the icy trough and wading through it was out of the question, so I hiked up the snow field along the stream until I found a snow bridge. It was about ten feet wide and appeared to be two feet thick, although the rushing water underneath was no doubt wearing it thinner by the minute. I studied it for several minutes. It looked fairly solid but there was no way to test it. I decided to take my chances and cross as quickly as I could. Heart pounding in my ears I hurried across, conscious of liquid ice rushing below and the hollow sound of my footsteps at the center of the bridge. I reached the other side in seconds. The snow bridge held. I could only wonder if it would still be there on my return.

I continued up the snowy slope. Visibility was deteriorating rapidly. Snow began falling hard enough to eventually obliterate my tracks. Without tracks for the descent my trip down the mountain would be most interesting.

I pressed on and the white field in front of me suddenly began to turn gray. The wind increased and gusted. I move ahead cautiously until I realized that the gray meant absence of mountain and presence of abyss. I had reached the summit and was right at the edge of a cliff.

Reaching the summit of a mountain is always a thrill. I recited a personal poem, said a prayer to the gods of the mountain and retraced my footsteps as best I could. My footprints were filling fast.

I developed a new personal rule for mountaineering in foul weather. When snow is falling from left to right, rather than vertically from the sky to the ground, it is time to go down.

It is the case that most accidents, falls and injuries occur on the descent. The climber is usually tired and with a pack the center of gravity is off making one unstable in all but the best footing. I slipped and slid, braced myself with the ice axe and quickly descended.

I reached the hollow snow bridge and carefully considered the risk of another crossing. I correctly reasoned the rushing ice water had probably weakened it even more in the last two hours. But how much? There was no way to tell. It had sounded very hollow on the first crossing. I took a few deep breaths and, heart thumping like a base drum, sprinted across the snow bridge, willing my feet to step as lightly as a humming bird, a difficult task when you feel more like an elephant. It was the longest fifteen seconds of my life. The bridge held.

I exhaled for what seemed like an eternity, then slowly descended to the meadows at the base of the mountain. On the way down the snow turned to sleet and the sleet turned to rain. Exhausted, I plopped down in a meadow and let soft rain fall on my face. I had made it to the top of the highest mountain in the United Kingdom.

After a few minutes I began to shake from the wet and cold and decided a warm place was in order. I drove to Fort William and stopped at the Volunteer Arms pub. My boots squished as I walked in. I set my daypack on the floor and dug into my pocket for some money. The publican took my order for a pint of the best and I placed a wad of very wet pound notes on the bar.

"Sorry, my money is all wet. I apologize."

"No need lad, we're used to wet ones here." He turned and with a clothespin, hung my money from a wire to dry.

There were just four of us in the Arms, the publican and two older local men, hunched over their pints, talking about fishing and football. The publican recognized my accent and inquired. "What brings you to Fort William?"

"Well, I've just climbed Mt. Ben Nevis in the rain. Reached the summit about two o'clock."

The publican looked at me with surprise. "You did it today, lad? In this?" He pointed to the rain falling outside the pub.

The two older gents looked up and one said, "So, you climbed the mountain in this weather?"

"Yes, I made it," I said with no small amount of pride. I waited, expecting to hear accolades for my bravery and grit.

"Well, lad," said the other older gent, "you'll be telling us which hospital you've escaped from. We'll be taken' you back now."

I put my head on the bar and laughed. And they all laughed with me.

Martha was a vision of lovely young Calendonian female and one not to be trifled with. As I entered the Craig Dhu I found her in front of the reception desk in a full length plaid skirt, shiny black shoes and an immaculate white blouse. By contrast I was pond scum on two legs.

She placed her hands on her hips and surveyed the conqueror of Ben Nevis. I stood there with a stupid grin on my face holding pack and ice axe and waiting for her to make a deduction.

"You did it then, did you?"

"Yes, indeed. Lovely day for a walk in the mountains," I said, the grin now impish.

"You must be wet through and through, Patrick, so you will be taking those wet things off at once." It was an order, not a suggestion.

I took the steps to my room only to discover Martha right behind me. "Hurry on now and get out of those awful things. Hurry."

I quickened my pace, reached the room and hurried in. Martha was hot on my heels. I looked at her, waiting for a question. No question.

"Right now, off with that wet stuff."

"Ah, Martha, I can do this but . . . " It was modesty and concern for the gross clothing that made me hesitate.

"But nonsense, get it off and give it to me and I'll have it laundered and ready to go in the morning."

"Martha, really, not necessary, I'll just pack it in my equipment bag and . . . ."

"No you won't, that'd be awful . . . . just give me these things. Hurry now, I've got plenty to do."

I began to strip off layers of wet and very gamey clothing. As fast as I took them off she grabbed and rolled them into a ball. I finally retreated to the privacy of the bathroom to take off the last layer and Martha's arm came through the small opening. She said, "Give 'em to me, for heaven's sake I've had four brothers, give me your under things." I did and she promptly disappeared. The site of this immaculately dressed young woman carrying my miserable layers of clothing was an incongruity I will not easily forget. She was oblivious, and as kind as one can imagine.

That night we celebrated in the wee pub. Much whiskey was consumed. I told and re-told the Ben Nevis story as the locals inquired. They took delight in the fact that an American would come all this way to climb Ben Nevis. Most of them had never been to the summit in their entire lives and had no interest in doing so. I've since learned that this is a norm, no matter where the mountain. Most locals do not go up.

Paddy, the big farmer, led the stories, Martha poured the scotch and I answered endless questions about the mountain and the United States. They were keenly interested in America.

By order of village law the pub officially closed, once again, and was promptly re-opened as a private bar a few moments later. This time Paddy did not have to restrain me from leaving.

I was proud of having climbed Ben Nevis solo and in terrible weather. They thought it a good feat as well. And then came the great equalizer. There is usually a great equalizer. One of the locals said, "Yes, Patrick, doing it in the weather is a challenge, but in good weather it is a lovely walk. Why many years ago, on a fair summer day, a lady from Edinburgh climbed it in high heels." Laughter.

"'Tis, nothing," said another local, "recall when Lord something-or-other drove his Model T Ford to the summit. Now that took some doin'." More laughter.

"And remember the time when a lad in his wheelchair pushed himself to the top while carrying a naked lady on his lap so he could keep abreast of his progress." Roars of laughter.

The stories came in droves, each more creative than the other. My ego resumed a proportionate size. They were letting me know that I had to keep my achievement in perspective. Humor is a great leveler.

"What's next, lad?" inquired Paddy the big farmer. I was impressed that he sensed there was a next. There was. I reached into my day pack and extracted my map of Mt. Kilimanjaro. I opened the map and spread it on the bar. The very name drew ohhs and ahhs for all had heard the exotic name Kil-a-man-jaro, but none in the room had ever been to Africa, much less up an African mountain.

"And when will you go, Patrick?"

I considered the question for the very first time. I had been over the map again and again since the purchase in Fort William. I cannot resist a map, particularly a great map. I looked at Martha and Paddy the big farmer, smiled and a voice, which sounded very much like mine, said, "Next year, I suppose."

So, we drank a toast to my intended climb of Mt. Kilimanjaro.

Then the American climber said, with a smile and a wink, "I think one should always make these momentous mountaineering decisions with a glass of scotch in hand and a mind free of inhibition and logic."

It had been a magic night. A night of celebration. A night of perspective and perhaps some leg pulling (a lady had climbed the damned mountain in high heels, I had been told). A night of warm friendship. And a night of new commitment. I had actually decided to climb Mt. Kilimanjaro, the highest mountain on the Continent of Africa, in a pub on a loch in the western highlands of Scotland. It must have been the local scotch.

I was the last to leave the pub. Martha turned out the light, gave me a warm kiss and wished me luck in Africa.

In the morning, as I checked out, I was handed a large package wrapped in plain brown paper, tied with white string. All my soaked and gritty clothing had been washed, ironed and properly folded. In Martha's fine hand was written, "Patrick. Safe Travels."

Let's Climb The Highest Mountain In Africa

Pushing through the crowd outside British customs at Gatwick Airport, I met my climbing partner, William C. Jackson. Bill had been in France with his brother, watching the French Open, touring the chateau country and suffering the cooking and the wine. He has a habit of accepting the tough assignments on the questionable premise that someone has to do them. Bill was smiling, pleased with our trans-Atlantic hook-up and happy to be queuing up for our first African adventure.

Bill is an extrovert of the first degree. He is about 6'1" runs a few pounds overweight, is a sandy haired California kid, Irish, fearless and the most opinionated person on the planet. There are no shades of gray in Bill's world. When he's on a roll, beating hell out of a subject, a position or an unsuspecting debate opponent, he reminds one of a loud and amplified Jack Nicholson. Perhaps it is the confidence instilled by the athletic department at the University of Nebraska. Bill was a full-ride tennis playing Cornhusker, and to hear him tell it, a damned good one. And he will tell it. When hubris gets a bit too thick for my taste I usually announce that Bill went to Nebraska, where sports takes precedent over academics. I cap this announcement by telling everyone within hearing distance that Bill thinks the "N" on the side of the football helmet stands for "knowledge." The ensuing laughter is generally an effective leveler . . . for a time.

Bill is an interesting traveling companion for he is extremely bright, lightening quick, sometimes too quick, has incredible breadth of knowledge, a wicked sense of humor and can be Don Juan or the very Devil in disguise. In essence, there is never a dull moment.

By contrast, I tend to be 5'9" if I stand up straight, an introvert with a secret desire to be an extrovert, an ever-curious observer, and sometime-diplomat.

It was good to be in London again. I had passed through London a year earlier on my way to do a solo climb of Mt. Ben Nevis. In Scotland I had acquired a map of Kilimanjaro. When I returned to the States I called Bill and mentioned the possibility of a climb of this storied mountain. It took Bill exactly one point five seconds to agree that it should be done.

It was comforting to know that we would have about two days in London before our long British Airways flight to Nairobi, Kenya and our attempt on Mt. Kilimanjaro. We would walk and stretch and dine and mentally prepare for the rigors of Africa.

Using the British Rail system and the London Underground we hustled off to an aging but relatively inexpensive hotel in Earl's Court.

Since we are both self-styled gourmands we decided that we must have at least one good meal. Bill had done some research and suggested Scott's in the ever so fashionable Mayfair section of London, not far from Grosvenor Square and the U.S. Embassy. It was, according to expert Jackson, the best sea food restaurant in London. I quizzed him on the atmosphere and he indicated many layers of linen, several forks, two wine glasses, a classic upper class bar in English leather, a separate champagne bar and staff in black tie. Scott's received an A.

I quizzed Bill on his wardrobe. He described every t-shirt he had ever accumulated, but no sport coat or blazer. Bill's plan for Africa was very creative. His modus operandi was to wear a t-shirt once. His modus vivendi was to launder no clothing in transit, to leave his t-shirts behind and lighten his load by the day. I explained that it would be difficult to get past the maitre d' at Scott's even in a starched and pressed white t-shirt and mountain boots. I always carry a navy blazer, one good shirt and a bow tie on every trip. This combination, I've found can take you from dinner in a nice restaurant to an audience with the Queen, without raising even a British eyebrow.

We stashed our gear and I directed our team to Bond Street where I knew we could find a blazer for the coat-less Jackson.

At Austin Reed I urged Bill to consider a double breasted navy blazer with gold buttons. With his height he was a natural for the double breasted look and it worked. I then lobbied for a British rep striped tie in navy, red and gold. He was almost convinced when he spotted a silk tie with elephants. The pull of an Africa he had never seen was too much, so elephants it was. We were now ready for a proper English dinner in Mayfair.

Our sartorial plan almost worked. We both discovered a major transgression. Shoes. In addition to Pivetta Italian mountain boots and Nike running shoes, I had a pair of Topsiders, a bit casual, but marginally acceptable. Bill had running shoes and newly broken in Danner mountain boots with heavy lug soles.

The classy maitre d' welcomed us like old friends, inquired about our presence in London and was genuinely impressed that we had chosen his restaurant for our last supper before Africa. "So, you are off to climb the famous Kilimanjaro are you? Then we shall take special care of you tonight." And he did.

The meal was a culinary triumph. Bombay gin on the rocks was served in crystal martini glasses, rimmed with a warm (note warm) lemon peel. Whole Dover sole, fresh from the channel, had been dusted lightly in flour (muinere) and sauteed in clarified butter. The fish arrived nutty brown and the waiter, after running the fish under our collective noses, quickly dissected it with the skill of a great surgeon, removed the bones, and reconstructed the delicious creature before our very eyes. The waiter then recommended a chilled, crisp French chardonnay which we accepted without hesitation. Two bottles later we decided it was indeed one of the best dining experiences we had ever enjoyed.

The maitre d' saw us to the door, wished us well on our climb of Kilimanjaro. He then asked several questions about mountaineering in general and Kili in particular. He was genuinely interested so we did our very best talk show. His final question was, "What makes a mountain ascent a true success in every sense." I touched his arm and said in a very serious tone, "The most successful mountain climbs are the ones we come back from." He hesitated for a split second and then saw the humor. As we said our final good byes he happened to glance down at our shoes and smiled. If you looked at us from the waist up we were almost jet set material.

There is a post script to this story. About four years later my friend and mentor Jim Carman, professor in the Haas Graduate School of Business, University of California at Berkeley, was serving as guest faculty at the London School of Business. Jim phoned from London and asked if I would consider crossing the Atlantic and addressing the students and faculty on leadership, service marketing and customer service in America. I was honored he would ask and I accepted immediately. Service quality, at the time, was an emerging concept in England and Jim thought my bloody noses and skinned knees from attempting to improve service in America would balance nicely with the academic principles he was teaching.

My wife Carol decided it was a good opportunity for a holiday. She spoke to our very dear buddies, Larry and Kathi Rambo in Wisconsin and soon the speaking invitation turned into a progressive party of international proportion. The Rambo's quickly agreed to join us. It would be their first trip outside the States.

Shortly after arriving in London we gathered for cocktails at the Carman's faculty residence which just happened to be in the Queen's former hunting palace facing Regent Park. It was an elegant beginning to a memorable evening. We commoners from The Colonies stood on the marble stairs overlooking the park and raised our martinis in salute to mother England and our good fortune.

Since we are all fond of excellent food and drink (Jim's wife Carol is a wonderful cook and Jim is a genuine wine connoisseur) we decided to seek a first class dining experience. I quickly suggested Scott's in Mayfair and intimated that it was the finest fish in the kingdom. All were impressed that the kid from the wrong side of the tracks in Wausau, Wisconsin would actually know of a Scott's. I tried to act nonchalant, as if I regularly dropped into London for cocktails and fashionable dining. But my ear-to-ear grin gave me away.

As we walked in, who should greet us but the maitre d' of my pre-African dining experience. I shook his hand and began to tell him I had previously been at Scott's on my way to Africa. He looked at me for a few seconds, smiled a knowing smile, cocked his head and said, "But of course, you chaps were on your way to climb Mt. Kilimanjaro."

I was astounded by his recall and complimented him on the quality of his memory. He then turned to my astonished friends and said, "You see, it isn't every day we have in our company gentlemen on their way to climb a famous mountain in Africa." He turned to me and smiled again, "I assume you had a successful climb of it?"

London, England
Sunday, May 31ˢᵗ

A Conversation With Dr. Samuel Johnson

Early on Sunday morning the streets and greens of central London were mostly still. We chose to walk east along River Thames to Blackfriars Bridge and on to Fleet Street. Fleet was once the home of British journalism and a much storied section of London. Reaching Fleet we passed the London Daily Mail, The Telegraph, Reuters, The Punch Pub (named for one of the world's longest surviving satirical magazines) and the offices of the BBC. We wandered and poked down alleys and into small court yards. Some of the buildings were older than our country.

An inspired Bill Jackson observed that 145 Fleet was once the address of one of England's greatest literary figures, Dr. Samuel Johnson. We located the entrance to 145 which proved to be an archway into a brick passageway. A few feet inside we found Ye Old Cheshire Cheese Pub. The Cheese is among the oldest of London's fabled public houses. More significantly, it is just steps away from Sam Johnson's house at 17 Gough Square.

If you write, even semi-seriously, or simply enjoy language, then Gough Square is a shrine. The white-washed home in which Johnson labored to produce the first dictionary, has been preserved. It lists more than a little to port, sagging from the ages, but it exists, a monument to the collection and interpretation of English words and the preservation of their meaning. In America, by contrast, we preserve the homes of politicians who do their level best to wring the least meaning out of words or obscure their meaning altogether.

I walked across the square and tried the door at Johnson's home. Finding it locked I retraced my steps to the pub. It became clear that Dr. Johnson could leave his writing table, out his door, walk through the courtyard, and take up residence in The Cheshire Cheese without exposing himself to the hustle and the stink of Fleet Street. In his day, the open London sewers once met on Fleet and the street of ink was something even more distinct.

The world's first lexicographer held court at The Cheese. The literary luminaries of the day and the political movers and shakers joined him for a pint or two.

We stood in the shadow of an adjacent building called Boswell House, admiring the historic pub which was also closed on Sunday morning. Many bright literary lights, thinkers, adventurers and at least one American President had raised a pint in The Cheshire Cheese: Alfred Lord Tennysen, Shelly, Keats, Mark Twain, Dickens, Teddy Roosevelt and James Boswell, Sam Johnson's biographer.

As I marveled at the scene I tried to imagine the lively discussions which must have taken place in The Cheshire Cheese in the Eighteenth Century. I'm sure Dr. Johnson's efforts were treated with some good natured skepticism. After all, there was no precedent for his plan to write a book describing every word in the English language. His friends and friendly detractors probably greeted his efforts with more than a little pub humor and spirited ridicule.

Step back in time, imagine a smoky, dark, candlelit room smelling of fermented brew and bubbling stew. And imagine the smiling faces and winks and nods as Johnson enters the room.

"Well, now, if it isn't the Gough Square man of words. How is the good Doctor Johnson this fine day?"

Johnson sits. "It would be fine if I were alone in this pitiful pub."

Groans from the assembled.

"Eh, Dr. Sam, how goes the book of words?"

Laughter from the assembled.

"Tedious, most tedious my dear fellow. A pint of your best please."

"Well, now Samuel, is this really fit work for an Oxford trained clerk?"

More laughter and some repeat the word "clerk." A few giggle.

"Don't pummel the clerks good fellow, many are capable of better writing than the likes of this besotted lot."

"Boo, hiss, unkind, Sam." More laughter from the crowd.

"Here now Johnson, what are you calling this . . . . this work-in-tedium?"

More laughter as the crowd begins to get into the tug and pull.

"Since a term with precedent is unavailable I shall invent a suitable nom. I'm at present considering the word . . . 'dic-tion-ary.'"

"Dic-tion-ary? Is it dick-shun-airy? Verrrrry impressive Sam . . . . I think."

Great laughter and the crowd begins to comment all at once.

"Dictionary, sounds a bit presumptuous."

"Hear, hear, a bit stuffy."

"A bit stuffed, I'd say."

"Nonsense, my limited friends. A dic-tion-ary shall be defined as a book listing a comprehensive selection of all the words in the English language. It shall contain the phonetic, grammatical and semantic value of each word. And I intend to miss not one . . . . you rabble."

"Rabble is it now? Why how, dear Johnson, would you be defining rabble?"

Roaring laughter. All eyes turn to Sam.

"That's it, that's it, how Johnson, would you define rabble? Oh, I cannot stand it, the laughing hurts . . . but tell us Sam, tell us please . . . . define rabble."

The entire room is laughing.

"I WILL DE FINE RABBLE . . . . slowly . . . to enable some of you to follow my remarks. Please note that the precise definition of 'rabble' contains many choices, HOWEVER . . . in this case I meant a LOW CLASS DISORDERLY MOB OF LIMITED INTELLIGENCE."

The room erupts with laughter. The chase is on and the exchange becomes high entertainment.

"Call it what you will, Johnson, but I wouldn't touch your dic-shun-ary with the French King's fork."

"Not worth a haypenny, Sam."

"Dic-shun-ary indeed, it sounds puffy."

"Puffy it is. Hear, hear, together now chaps, PUFF! PUFF! PUFF!"

"After allllll, Dr. Samuel, it is to be merely a novelty, not so? I mean, surely no one can expect a mere Gough Square mortal such as ye, even one who has sloughed thru the pubs of Oxford, to successfully describe evvvveerrrry word used in Britain. Surely not?"

Johnson rises, pint in hand. "HUSH DULLARD! My dictionary will be more than a novelty. It may even enable the likes of you to understand and be well understood, although a pint does make me optimistic."

"Dullard, is it? Now, how would your dic-shun-ary be describing 'dullard?'"

Laughter and then silence. Johnson scans the room.

"According to my dictionary, a dullard is an IDIOT."

"And how does the dic-shun-ary describe idiot?"

"My dictionary describes idiot as anyone living north of Hadrian's Wall."

Gasps from the assembled, followed by silence.

"But, Sam . . . . that's . . . . why that's SCOTLAND."

"Congratulations young man. Pints for all."

Taking The Tube To Nairobi

From our Earl's Court hotel it is just two colorful blocks to the Tube, the efficient London Underground system. We deposited a pound and forty, popped through the gate and we were off to Heathrow airport.

The train chattered and creaked through the city and into the countryside, passing endless rows of neat brick homes, each with a postage stamp garden. There were many stops in route and one very memorable stop for a lad named Punch.

Three young gentlemen were heading home from a Sunday in the center of London. The rhythm of the train and a few pints put a lad named Punch to sleep. Just before the home stop his two companions rose and very quietly, taking great care not to wake him, made their way past Punch to the door. When the train stopped they ran out on the platform and waited at the window of the train, just inches from the sleeping unsuspecting Punch. When the doors closed and the train began to move they pounded on the window.

Punch was jolted by the sound, his head snapped and his eyes opened. He was dazed, but aware that the train was moving. He leaped up, shouting a curse, threw himself at the automatic doors and attempted to force them apart. Too late. The train was now moving swiftly out of his home station. He cursed again as the two laughing faces of his buds tried to keep pace with the train and one last look at the angered and deflated Punch.

"Bastards," was all he could mumble through clenched teeth, "bloody bastards." He retreated to his seat and avoided all glances. We were smiling, he was not. Should we have warned him? Perhaps. Then again, we would have ruined a perfectly good practical joke and they would have had one less story to tell and re-tell at the local pub.

The second Tube of the day was a Boeing 747, British Air flight 55, London to Nairobi, Kenya. Wheels were up at 8:15 PM. We would fly through night and arrive in East Africa on Monday morning.

There have been few traditions in my life. Mumm champagne, however, is a tradition. When significant things have happened or been achieved I have purchased a fifth of G. H. Mumm Cordon Rouge, savored the victory and every last yeasty bubble. While there have been some poor times in a monetary sense, I have somehow always found the means for a Mumm

The tradition began when the U. S. Army released me from a life altering experience they call Advanced Infantry Training. A chartered aircraft took about one hundred of us young, fit, trained killers to O'Hare Field in Chicago. In civilian clothes and with a pocketful of money I decided to spend the weekend in the Windy City, one of my favorite places. On an impulse I entered a wine shop on Rush Street and a kindly gentleman decided I should celebrate my Army graduation with a bottle of champagne. He recommended G. H. Mumm. That evening I celebrated in my hotel room with a chilled bottle of crisp, yeasty Mumm and a thin crust cheese pizza. As author Harry Golden would have said, "Only in America."

Earlier, in a college literature course, I learned the rich, the famous and the infamous, in Somerset Maugham novels, sipped Mumm as they plotted, confided, cohabited, conjoined and celebrated. How civilized of Maugham to put Mumm in hand. I marveled at how much I had learned from literature.

Imagine my delight when I discovered that British Airlines had included chilled Mumm on their drink trolley. It seemed perfectly fitting to toast a first departure for Africa and The mountain with Mumm. It was cold and dry and traveled very well.

Independence Day In Kenya

The African morning was cool. Even a click or two south of the Equator the air can be cool. Why was I surprised? Perhaps it was the image of a steamy, tropical Africa I had learned at the movies. Old stereotypes are difficult to overcome. The cool crisp air was invigorating.

Passing through customs at Jomo Kenyatta Airport it was impossible to miss the Kenyan soldiers in camouflage battle dress. It was also disturbing to note they were carrying loaded rifles. Even though their expressions were blank with boredom, like guards the world over with little to guard, the effect was chilling enough. I had served in the Army and knew the stopping power of their weapons. Welcome to Kenya.

Since this was a do-it-yourself expedition (no Abercrombie and Kent Safari Tour for us) I went to collect our rented vehicle while Bill went to the Central Bank branch to exchange some form of money into Kenyan shillings. At this stage in the journey Bill had francs, pounds and dollars. The rate of exchange proved to be about 100 shillings for seven American dollars. The act of changing money became a rolling challenge as the trip unfolded.

I had arranged for the rental of a four wheel drive truck for our trip across the back roads of the Great Rift Valley to Tanzania and the shadow of Kilimanjaro. The truck, an Isuzu Trooper II, was a tough, stiff, four wheeler. Our model had wire cages over the head lamps and a heavy duty spare locked to the tailgate. The steering wheel was on the right and one drives on the left in Kenya. While the vehicle design was rather British, the traffic was decidedly French, frenetic and about as orderly as a herd of rabbits. When Bill volunteered to drive the first leg in Nairobi rush hour traffic it took only the shortest of seconds for me to hand him the keys.

The Norfolk Hotel

Since we had no feeling for the comfort of the ground or just how many nights we would be sleeping on it we decided to be kind to our jet lagged bodies and spend the first night in a good hotel. Prior to boarding the 747 in London we met a distinguished looking import executive with a great deal of African travel experience. He recognized that it was our first trip to Africa, considered several hotels and then wisely suggested The Norfolk.

The Norfolk Hotel is a slice of British colonial history. Apparently it was "the club" for English pioneers who developed this portion of East Africa. The Norfolk occupies several acres on the edge of the University of Nairobi campus. Present management we noted was taking pains to preserve this example of the heritage and ambiance of colonial Kenya.

The Hotel is a series of buildings forming a large, rectangular compound. In the middle of the hotel grounds there are large trees with wire pens at the base which contain a colorful collections of birds. Antique carriages, motor cars and farm implements are displayed nearby on carefully tended lawns.

The rear "wall" of the compound is the original hotel building, circa 1930. On this day the whitewashed façade contrasted sharply with the bright green lawn and the clear blue sky. One expected, at any moment, a Dennis Finch Hatten, Ernest Hemingway or Dr. Livingston to amble out in kahki bush dress, ready for a day of hunt or adventure on the plains.

Native chefs in starched white uniforms wearing tall white toques, criss-crossed the grounds, moving between a central kitchen and several dining areas. I watched the parade from a second floor roof top deck and smiled at our good fortune. There was nothing American or plastic about The Norfolk.

As I gazed down through the trees it took little creative effort to imagine a colonial wedding reception, a family reunion, a picnic for horse trainers with Beryl Markham on her father's arm, a meeting of Royal physicians, or a reception for a British Prince or MP. On the lawns below I was certain a tear had been shed for someone dying too soon in the harsh climate of this wild land. Or tears of joy, perhaps, for a bountiful crop, or a new born settler. All celebrated on the greens of The Norfolk.

Nairobi—Adjusting To Another Culture

It was Kenyan Independence Day. Americans can relate. Independence is what our country is all about. We celebrate American Independence Day on July 4th with gusto, snap, crackle, pop and passion.

We decided to do a walking tour of the center of the Kenyan capitol city. I'm not sure if it was jet lag, the interruption of circadian rhythms, a lack of African experience or little exposure to conditions in developing nations, but we were very disappointed.

I did my best to keep things in perspective. I thought how visitors to the United States must feel when they see contrasts between wealth and poverty in one of the most prosperous nation's on the planet. It is possible, for example, to view the splendor of the White House in Washington, DC and, in a few blocks, step over a homeless person huddling for some small comfort on a piece of cardboard near a warm air vent in the sidewalk.

Nairobi was depressing.

Within a few chipped, cracked, worn and dirty blocks of the Kenyan capitol building I watched natives picking through piles of garbage strewn across an alley behind a restaurant. The garbage had been there a while.

From a distance the capitol building looked like a modern tower, designed to mimic the trunk of an ancient giant scenecio tree. It is earth toned and contemporary and reminds one of the Capitol Records building in Hollywood. Up close it is dirty and forlorn. Sad.

Even the new buildings in Nairobi seemed old, as if built with used materials.

A fine layer of red dust coated much of the city, adding to the drab, dull appearance of shops and office buildings.

And the people? There was no joy in the faces we saw. There was little eye contact between Kenyan and American, no communication and no visible, friendly spirit in the city. This was Independence Day?

Were we that different, I wondered, as we walked block after dusty block? Was it wrong to apply our feelings to the scene? Were we so anesthetized by our long standing prosperity and independence that we were missing a point? Or was Kenyan Independence Day a celebration of a very limited and fragile freedom?

We walked back to The Norfolk Hotel in silence. There is something wrong with this scene, I concluded. Something very wrong. Language may be a barrier, but human expression, human spirit usually transcends the gap. A smile, for example, translates into any language in the world. It means the same thing in every culture. We saw no smiles. None. We saw no joy of independence and freedom. We could hear no celebration.

And we had the answer.

Nairobi To The Amboseli
Tuesday, June 2nd

Looking For A Snow Capped Mountain At The Equator

The uniformed guard gave us an open palm British Army salute as we nosed the truck out of the secure Norfolk Hotel compound. I returned a razor sharp American Army salute and we headed south to Tanzania in search of Mt. Kilimanjaro.

Our plan was to cross a section of the Great Rift Valley, which curves through the center of East Africa. My map indicated there was a major highway between Nairobi and the border with Tanzania. We estimated a day of easy driving and our spirits were high. Naiveté will do that to you every time.

Our destination was the Amboseli National Park, a Kenyan game reserve which hugs the border with Tanzania and offers great views of Kilimanjaro. Our intent was to photograph the mountain from the north side, sleep on the ground, view the animal herds in the reserve on Wednesday morning, cross the border into Tanzania and continue to the base of the mountain to prepare for a climb on Thursday. It did not seem like an ambitious plan.

Kenyan highways carry an "A," "B," or "C" prefix. We left Nairobi on A104/109. An "A" road, I assumed, was a super highway. Never assume. The street in front of your home is superior in width and quality to the best "A" road in Kenya. As we bounced along we silently speculated that if this was an "A" then God help us on a "C."

Bill offered to drive the first day, so I read the map and looked for highway signs. I discovered that looking for highway signs was almost as difficult as tracking wild game on hard ground. The signs either don't exist or are very small (think broken twig or bent grass).

The "A" road we were on split at some point, one branch heading south to the Amboseli the other heading east to Mombassa and the Indian Ocean. We wanted south. After a few hours my compass said "east" and I determined that we were somehow on the road to

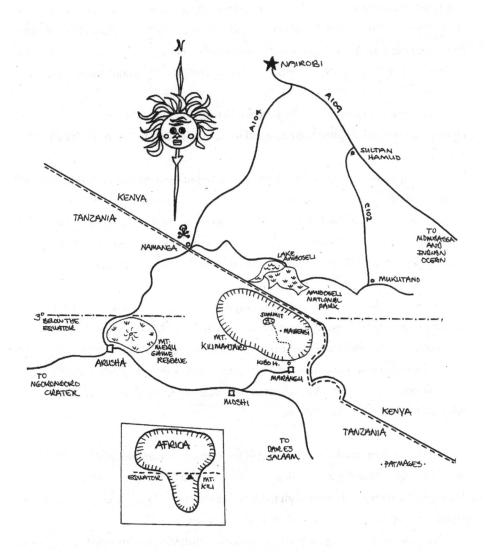

Mombassa, which sounds like the title of a Hope-Crosby motion picture. Our mountain was clearly in another direction. Somehow we had missed the fork in the road. The score was Africa 1, American expedition nil.

What African road organization failed to give us we got from Scotland cartographers. My two pound purchase in Fort William a year earlier suggested there was a back road to the Ambolseli. A "C" road, C102, would take us from a town called Sultan Hamud to Makutano and a hard right would take us into the Amboseli Reserve and give us views of the great mountain. We motored on with confidence and resolve. What you don't know is almost an anesthetic.

Sultan Hamud turned out to be a British Petroleum pump, a broken down bus, a few chickens, a store with a rusted Coke sign and no door or glass in the windows. We could not find C102.

Fighting all my American male genes (real men don't stop to ask for directions as real women certainly know) I walked into the store, prepared to savor a cold coke and good information. It was dark. Pitch black, in fact. A voice spoke. I asked for "Coke." I heard what I thought was "No." I asked for "C102." I heard what I thought was "Get the hell out of here and be quick about it." There was just something about the voice that persuaded me to return to the truck.

We drove back and forth, searching for any sign of a road south. The only visible sign of anything even remotely resembling a road was a rut of tire tracks in the red soil. Could this be the line on my map which continued for 100 miles to the game reserve? I shouted to a native walking along the road and pointed in the direction of the tire tracks, "Mukutano?" And he waved us on. We turned off the highway and drove down the track in disbelief and with a helluva lot less resolve and confidence.

The ruts and tire tracks took us through the village of Sultan Hamud. It was about one city block long and consisted of small sagging little wooden buildings resembling store fronts. They were weathered and coated with red dust. Windows and doors were open, I assume to capture any and all suggestions of a breeze or puff of air.

The product of the village seemed to be colorful short African skirts called kangas. As we passed we waved at natives milling in the main street (read dirt road), many waved back. The scene was bleak save for one splash of intense color, a small display of kangas on a rickety wooden frame. It was a spot of red, yellow, green and pink on a canvas of dull grey.

As we motored past the last building I saw an old, round shouldered man, wrinkled, bare to the waist, eyes half closed, slumped in a rickety chair. His hands were working an ancient sewing machine. Only his hands and his yellowed, bleary eyes moved as he guided bright cloth and watched us as we moved out of his village.

The vision was lasting. The sewing machine was exactly like the one my grandmother had used, the kind you operated by pushing a trundle with your feet to make the needle go up and down and pierce the cloth with thread. It was, as I recall of the mid 1940's, the most high tech piece of equipment in her house. No electricity required. Just push with your feet and create your very own fashion. The sewing machine, operated by the soft and talented hands of my grandmother, Lyda Mages was the source of endless fascination for a curious three year old grandson. Forty-three years later the machine continued to fascinate the grandson, but in the hands of an ancient African grandfather stitching together the fabric of his life.

But the man. The wiry black hair, tinged with grey, sad yellowing eyes, the slump of old and weary shoulders and the curve of his bare back spoke volumes of life on the plains of Africa. If there was any fascination for him in the trundle driven sewing machine it did not show. His eyes said nothing. His soul was not connected to his face.

I can still see him.

We bumped along, the drone of the engine only interrupted by an occasional "shit" or "sonovabitch" as the truck hit a deeper rut than the last. We motored along at the speed the road would allow, about twenty miles per hour with spurts to thirty. The terrain was so bleak and stark that I asked Bill to stop so I might make a Kodachrome or two.

It was at this point in our journey that I finally saw Africa. With feet planted firmly on the dusty soil I was able to feel Africa and eyeball a panorama of little and nothing . . . . but great and grand.

The plain was endless. In every direction there was horizon. More sky than I have ever seen. The dots on the plain were small scrub bushes. The only trees were short acacia trees which resembled the December trees of my Wisconsin youth.

Our road was the only mark. It appeared to be a long dusty ribbon, frayed and wrinkled and endless. The road seemed to be going nowhere and there seemed nowhere to go . . . but on.

We drove for hours on this white track seeing everything and nothing but soil and sky and sky and sky. I ran all kinds of words through my head . . . . big, huge, grand, vast. None of the words had the right stuff, and I concluded that my vocabulary was truly half-vast.

Late in the afternoon we met very small, spindly Masai children in their simple brown capes. It was hard to determine their age. I guessed six or seven, but they were working a herd of skinny cattle, the family wealth, with sharply pointed sticks. As we approached they lined the road and some of them waved. Every one of their big brown eyes were on this oddity in their barren world—two white men in a shiny white truck. The contrast was palpable. They had brown capes, pointed sticks and very thin cattle. We had a truck filled with down sleeping bags, many changes of clean clothes, more t-shirts than they would own in a lifetime, bottled French water, high tech mountain tent, cameras, powdered swiss soups, credit cards, water purification pills, and a first aid kit that was more modern medicine than they had ever experienced. We certainly had the right material stuff, but they were smiling and we were not.

As I watched them wave it occurred to me that we had traveled on four continents in our short lifetime and would probably live to travel at least two more before our mountaineering days were over. They would be herding cattle and goats the rest of their days and, quite possibly, on the same stretch of plain. Yet they were smiling and we were not.

In their teens they would graduate from pointed sticks to modest spears, void of any ornamentation. When the boys reached manhood, if they reached manhood, they would acquire a spear with an iron blade on one end and an iron cattle prod on the other. If they excelled as men they would earn a multi-bladed killing spear, the symbol of the hunter, the very spear that took on lion and other major game. But as they grew older the spears would gradually become more simple until, when old and bent, they would finally carry the old man's spear . . . a sharply pointed stick . . . just like the stick carried by children. It was a poignant and unmistakable cycle.

The greatest challenge for the children would be staying alive in a landscape that offered little except space to walk and air to breathe. But they were smiling.

We waved and drove on. It was late afternoon and we appeared to be very far from our objective. In spite of the hour and the need to press on we stopped to make a photograph of a young Masai herding what appeared to be about 100 head of cattle in a single file. Red dust billowed and swirled into the sky. The scene was back lit by a sun low in the sky. Everything was red and orange and shades of warm I had never seen. It was a vision photographers live for.

I quickly clamped a telephoto lens on my Nikon and braced on the hood of the truck. The cattle were black and dark grey shadows, heads down, plodding home, framed by red African dust. My heart was pounding in my ears. The scene was ancient, authentic and beautiful.

In the corner of the frame I noticed something moving at high speed. It was the Masai, spear in hand, running across the plain directly toward us and closing fast. It didn't feel right.

I flashed on the thought that some natives fear the camera, something about taking their soul. An insult. Perhaps an outrage.

We had no collective experience with Masai herdsmen. We didn't speak Swahili. We had never dealt with a sharp spear. The learning curve on this one looked long and slow. We processed hard and both arrived at the same conclusion, quickly and without discussion.

"We're out'a here, big guy."

"Hit it, Mr. Jackson, if you please."

We pulled away as fast as the Trooper would pull. The native continued running at us.

"He is fast, very, very fast."

"Wisconsin Badger running back material, no question."

"With all the dust, definitely Big Ten."

I looked back and the horizon was obscured by swirling dust.

We had been driving all day, mile after barren mile, bleak yet beautiful. We had not seen anything that looked remotely like a settlement. The map indicated a right turn at the village of Mukutano. But where was Mukutano? We motored on fearful of losing the light before we reached the Amboseli game reserve.

On the left a small group of wooden buildings appeared, but no community. It looked like a family homestead, but certainly not a village. No sign of life. Could this be Mukutano? We both shrugged and on instinct turned right, the stuff of adventure.

After some calculation it seemed to me that Kilimanjaro should be in sight. We began searching the horizon for Kili, hoping to get a sighting before nightfall. The horizon, due south according to our compass, remained clear. No mountain. We pressed on.

C'mon, I silently pleaded, you can't hide a 19,000 foot mountain. There are no foothills, no build up to Kilimanjaro. It is a volcano that just popped out of the plains. It is the only big mountain in this part of the world. The only one. So, where is it?

Search. Scan. I found myself hunched forward only inches from the windshield. No mountain in sight.

Questions began building. The worst thing that can happen to intrepid explorers, especially amateur intrepid explorers, happened . . . we began to lose confidence. Could we possibly be that far off? We had excellent maps and proper direction, confirmed by compass headings. There is only one road and it goes south, straight at the mountain. Are distances that deceiving? I recalculated mileage and speed. It fit. No errors. We should be in sight of the famous snow capped mountain at the equator. The very mountain early scientists said could not exist. How, they reasoned, could snow exist at the equator?

Where is the mountain? Perhaps it's hidden in the clouds? We were warned that Kili is covered with clouds most of the year. It makes its own weather.

Bill and I began exchanging grumbles. So, I called "time out" and counseled patience. "Look, if we fail to reach the game reserve, if we fail to see the mountain, we will simply stop the truck at nightfall, pitch our tent, make some hot soup and call it a day. Rest will do wonders and we will push on in the morning at first light." Neither of us were placated or convinced by my simple deduction. We were frustrated but we clearly understood that frustration can lead to very bad decisions.

We searched the horizon. The light continued to fade and, as evening shadows grew longer, a thick layer of clouds appeared on the horizon directly in our path. They held the dazzling pink rays of a setting sun.

German explorers reported a snow capped mountain at the equator as early as the nineteenth century. Colleagues in Europe laughed long and loud. A snow capped mountain at the equator, indeed! The reports were ridiculed and rejected until photography was invented and images were made, confirming that the Germans had not been high on African beer or fried by the heat at the equator.

We pressed on, windows open and we now shivered in the cold evening air. We searched the sky for a clue, for the moon, for something. The tension, the constant pitching and bouncing of the truck was now painful. We had been riding a bucking bronco all day long.

"Stop, Bill, stop the truck. Let's stretch a bit and talk this over."

After a little stretching and pacing I decided to climb up on the hood of the truck and rest my back against the windshield. The warmth of the engine radiating through the hood of the truck was a comfort. I tilted my head back to ease the tension in my neck. I rolled my head from side to side and looked at the fleeting clouds moving east. Then I noticed a white cloud that wasn't moving. It took my brain a few seconds to analyze the image. And then my heart skipped a beat. There it was, poking through the clouds. I had found the mountain.

We stared up in disbelief. The feeling was shock, followed by awe, followed by dumb smiles. There it was, the summit of Kilimajaro. It was there all along, but it was higher than we had expected to find it. We had been looking too low, searching the horizon for mountains we were used to seeing, 10,000 or 12,000 foot mountains in the United States. We were not looking high enough. The summit of Kili was more than a mile higher than any mountain we had ever climbed; higher than any mountain we had ever seen.

We stood on the silent plain and just stared at the snow cap in the clouds. Because of the dust in the air it was not possible to see the shoulders of the mountain. The shoulders of the mountain might be twenty miles wide, perhaps more. We couldn't see the outline of the mountain for the haze. But we could finally see the top poking through the clouds. It was, indeed, a snow capped mountain, glaciated in fact. The sheer scale of Africa had overwhelmed our conventional view of terrain and mountains. It now made sense. The mountain was there all along. Our navigation was accurate, the maps were true. Africa two, American expedition, nil.

Bill walked away from the truck and out on the barren African plain. He walked toward the mountain in the fading light. His hands were pressed into his pockets, shoulders hunched against the chill. He turned in the dusk and I could see the smile on his face.

Sitting in the semi-darkness of this ghostly, windswept plain, actually shivering at the equator, I at once felt the raw excitement of simply viewing a mountain this big. And I also felt a tingle of fear that goes along with a climb this high . . . . a climb higher than the heavens.

One presumes there were angels in the cloud filled heavens who were also looking up at the mountain. Perhaps they too were wondering if they had enough warm clothes, enough water, and enough will to climb to the top. Surely wings don't work that high.

Would we actually stand there, above the clouds, on the frozen white cap of the very top of Africa? Was it possible?

Crossing The Amboseli At Night—Please Try To Avoid Hitting The Elephants

In prep for this trip we had been told not to drive the plains at night. On our first night we found ourselves driving the plains. We bumped along the ruts and the tracks as best we could, straining to see signs of life. Eventually we found the entrance to the Amboseli Reserve. In the blue-grey mist of headlights and dust we saw what appeared to be barracks for the park guards. Bill pulled the truck to a stop in front of what looked like a set from a "B" movie. A tacky guard house squatted next to the tire tracks that passed for the road. A fragile gate with a single bar pretended to block the way.

As my eyes grew accustomed to the dark I began to smile. It was clear that nothing but air space and a steering wheel prevented a driver from turning right and going around the little gate.

In fact, if one turned right one could no doubt drive a hundred miles and not encounter another barrier. It was humorous. I giggled. Then looked for stage braces behind the wall of the guard house. Surly this was a movie set, it couldn't be a real building. We sat in the dark and waited for a challenge from a park guard. We waited quite a while.

"Bill, this must be the place where they send the Kenyan guards who fall from favor." We both laughed.

Bill got out of the truck and approached the pitch dark guard house. "Hello. Anyone home?"

A soft voice from the shadows said, "Closed, it closed, too late, nothing can be done."

Bill laughed and turned to me. "Hey, Mage, hear that? It's closed, the park is closed and nothing can be done."

Hundreds of square miles of endless open space is closed. A fragile little gate barely blocked the width of the tire tracks. The scene reminded me of a Gary Larson cartoon. This was the "Far Side."

I pictured lions, elephants, and wildebeest with their feet up in lazy-boy recliners, reading the Nairobi Standard and sipping their first dry gin of the evening (over ice with a lemon twist, stirred not shaken, thank you) after a long hard day of working the plain. Their day was in, the animals had punched out and wouldn't return till 7:00AM Wednesday morning—union rules.

I could make out the expression on Bill's face. In situations like this he takes on a Cheshire Cat grin, a cross between Jack Nicholson and the Devil.

"Well, gee, were sorry that you're closed. I guess if we can't go on to the hunting lodge and a bed then we'll have to sleep here, right outside your gate. That's OK isn't it?"

No, I thought, that isn't OK. Another no-no is to pitch a tent on the ground where the beasts working on the night shift will find you during their hunt and enjoy human ala cart. I said nothing and listened to the negotiation.

The soft voice from the guard house said, "Nothing can be done. No, no."

Silence. Soft voice again. "You have tent?"

"Yeah, sure, we have tent, sleeping bags, food, water and fire. We'll sleep here on the ground. OK?"

Silence. Long silence. Bill and I conferred.

"William, I don't think they want us on their front steps, clearly we are a complication. God knows what games are played here at night. Let's press him to let us pass and take our chances in the dark."

Bill agreed and said to the guard house, "Tell you what, how about we just go into the park and try to find the lodge. That's a better deal for everyone."

Silence.

Soft voice from the guard house: "Closed. Nothing can be done." Pause. "You have shillings?"

"Sure."

"You have two hundred shillings?"

"Yeah, sure, we have two hundred."

Silence, but not as much silence.

"You go. Not stay here. You go and hurry, hurry to lodge. Not to drive in the park after dark. You go now. Hurry." The hand came out of the dark, Bill handed the shillings, the hand retracted. We waited for a ticket or a receipt. Silence. No movement. We waited in the truck, engine idling, for the gate to go up. Nothing happened. Finally, Bill put the truck in reverse, backed up about ten feet, cranked the steering wheel to the right and we drove around the little gate, with miles to spare. The park was closed.

"We never did see his face," Bill observed, "all I ever saw was a hand taking the money."

"Well, William, the lesson is clear, Jesse James wore a mask. Kenyan guards wear the dark."

I am compelled to digress from our passage into the closed park and teach a brief course in official African logic. This is not to be confused with native African logic. I'm referring to the logic of officials, the people with a uniform, a rubber stamp and a little authority. It is an ordered pattern of thought which has an amazingly consistent deduction and outcome.

1.   You cannot do that. (No reason proffered).
2.   Nothing can be done. No, no, no.
3.   You have shillings?
4.   Maybe something can be done. Not good. We see.
5.   You have dollars?
6.   OK, you go. Hurry.

This is not intended as criticism of African people. It is a well aimed shot at African officials. I have concluded there should be a separate country in Africa for all officials. They should be herded into a special reserve so as to restore the continent to its original splendor. I would contribute the first dollar, a crate of rubber stamps and even design their flags and uniforms in several interchangeable shades of currency green. They could say "no" and stamp to their heart's content, and leave humanity alone, so many something's could be done.

We left the closed back gate of the Amboseli, happy to have at least a chance at finding the hunting lodge (now a hotel) and a safe place to sleep. It was dark. About as dark as it can get.

Driving in the pitch black of African night was a new experience. There was no light anywhere, save for our headlights. The scene in our windshield was monochromatic. Everything looked gray and the same. It was ever harder to see the faint tire tracks we were doing our best to follow. After a tiresome hour of strained eyes and bumps and lumps from the ruts in the road we detected faint lights on the horizon. Much to our delight they began to get bigger and brighter. We pressed on, rocking and rolling, eyes straining. Suddenly what road there was became wet, then mushy and then water. Bill quickly put the truck in reverse, backed up and then turned left until the tires found solid ground. Evidently we were on the edge of a large watering hole or a small lake. Hearts speeded up and then settled down. We continued our detour and much to our chagrin the lights on the horizon began to fade. We were tacking away from the oasis and not liking it a bit.

Turn, twist, bump, brake, accelerate, change gears, bump again. Where would it end, when would it end? Tired. Very tired. Vincent T. Lombardi, the fabled football coach was right, fatigue makes cowards of us all. Want to stop. Even pitch a tent in the dark and roll up in a sleeping bag. Take a chance on the animals. Smear a little engine oil or petrol on our skin to dissuade them. Want sleep. Want rest. Want to stop wearing this truck. Have had it. Africa is winning.

Bump, twist, downshift, accelerate, brake and bump again.

I lost track of the number of times my head hit the roof of the truck on the up side of a rut, or hit the window of the truck on the downside of a rut. I graduated from "damn it" to "sonofabitch" to language I cannot report.

"Jeez, Bill, on the left, lookout!!!!"

Suddenly all senses returned, switched on, all systems on full alert.

"What the hell is it?" We both strained to see dark shadows in front of the truck.

"Eyes, mygod, lots of yellow eyes, dozens . . . . hundreds."

"What have we got."

"Dunno, do not know . . . . go slow, go slow."

Bill downshifted quickly and pumped the brakes. We both snapped door locks as we moved forward, slowly, cautiously.

A mass of animals with yellow eyes came into the dim beams of our headlights.

A herd of wildebeest plodded past our truck, sweeping around us at a safe distance, barely touching our truck. They looked like small buffalo and behaved like nervous cows. This parade lasted for five minutes and, once clear of the herd, we tried in vain to pick up the tire tracks. But our elusive African trail had been effectively obliterated by thousands of wildebeest hooves. Never at a loss for humor, someone in the truck said, "Damned un-wieldy beasts."

But humor did not play well and we continued to probe the darkness, searching for tire tracks or ruts that would lead us to food, drink and beds.

Just moments after the passing of the unwieldy-beasts, Bill once again braked hard. Just ahead of us our headlights picked up a single pair of red eyes. The red eyes were not moving and were fixed on our truck.

"What? What have we got?

"Can't tell yet, roll the windows up."

Four white eyes strained to cut through the dark and decide just how afraid to be.

"It's got to be a cat of some type."

"Right, the cat that follows the herd looking for supper."

We passed within twenty feet of a lone hyena, part of the dominant end of the African food chain. The hunter, never the hunted.

The hyena watched us pass. We resembled Tom Wolfe's description of the early astronauts, "Spam in a can." The truck body had become aluminum foil, thin aluminum foil. The windows were now Saran wrap. We too, after all, were meat, white meat. But this night the lame or the slow wildebeest was the main course, so the hyena resumed the hunt.

We continued on, damp with sweat and weary to the bone.

"On the right, is it rock?" Bill swerved left.

"Don't know, could we be at the base of the mountain?"

"No were not that close . . . . look out on the left, big something."

Bill pulled the wheel cautiously to the right and a tusk flashed past my window.

"Elephants! Elephants! . . . . damn, we have elephants."

"Big elephants, lots of elephants."

We stopped and they moved closer. Instinctively, Bill, who had little experience driving in elephant herds and even less experience driving through them in the dark, began to accelerate slowly and we cautiously worked our way through the grazing herd.

I felt a combination of awe and fear. Even in the dark, they were incredible animals. Imagine looking out your window and seeing a knee. Or the bottom of a tusk. Or the lower lobe of a flapping ear. Truly awesome. Then imagine hitting one or angering a bull and you have sphincter tightening fear.

As we passed the last of the elephants, we reached the edge of a gully and began an uncertain descent. The truck rocked, rolled and stuttered and we bounced from side to side. My head hit the window, then the truck bucked to the right, which threw me toward Bill, and then we bucked to the left again and I met the glass once more. I threw my arms up like a punch drunk fighter, struggling through the last round and hit the window once again.

It felt as if we were in a giant pinball machine, the kind I loved to play as a kid. Unwieldy-beasts on the left, hyena on the right, elephants fore and aft, bonus points if you missed them, no bumper guards and you cannot use the flippers. Miss them, react, don't think, just avoid them and for heaven's sake don't "tilt" the machine, I'm out of quarters.

Motoring through the Amboseli Game Reserve at night is best avoided. It is exceedingly difficult to drive in an elephant herd. The swerving and cursing disturbs the animals and makes them very unfriendly.

How we managed to drive through an elephant herd in the dark without bumping an elephant is difficult to comprehend. Does luck count? Of course it does.

The nose of the truck turned up and we began negotiating the other side of a great gully. As we emerged at the top we found what appeared to be a heavily traveled dirt track.

"This must be the main road, the ruts are deeper." We laughed.

"Right or left?"

"Without a map, a compass, or light the rule is to be right, go right."

"Now where in hell did you pick that up?" said a curious Bill Jackson.

"Made it up just now . . . go right. No sign, so we steer with our gut."

For the next few moments we drove on in silence, not sharing private thoughts or startling images of wildebeest, hyena or elephants. Breathing was almost back to normal, but the perspiration that soaked our bush clothes was now cold and clammy. We were both numb.

We learned that it is not wise to drive the African plains at night. We learned that wildebeest eyes are yellow, hyena eyes are red and slow or lame wildebeest are dead.

I've never hit an elephant, only a whitetail deer. I managed this unfortunate trick in a white Volkswagen Beetle. The Volks turned red, venison all over the place . . . . and not a lump of butter or an onion in sight. I did a proper job of it, kept the car on the snow covered road somehow and dispatched the deer express air into a frozen corn field. But an elephant? What happens if you hit an elephant? Do you bounce off and motor on? No, that's the stuff of a cartoon. Does the elephant take exception and compress your vehicle into four cubic feet of steel and tourist? Do you call the Kenyan park guards? No, they will want shillings or dollars. Do you stop and exchange names and insurance companies?

"Yes, State Farm, I just hit an elephant. Elephant's OK, but we're in extremis. Their company? Sorry, didn't ask Our deductible? How about deducting one truck and two mountaineers."

Where is Marlin Perkins when you really need him?

Bill hit the brakes and I bumped the windshield.

Grey African dust boiled around the skidding truck. Seat belts strained, heads snapped and bobbed.

Lions. One, two . . . . three lions emerged from the dark and slowly, ever so slowly slinked across the road directly in front of the truck. It was like a dream sequence in a movie. Clouds of dust like theatrical smoke drifted in the wind and big cats, female, paraded before us. They were truly beautiful, regal, heads held high, necks erect pulling scents from the air and crossing right in front of us.

Deadly, wild, fluid beauty.

There was absolutely nothing to do. It was their world. We intruded. Are we the menu or simply the spectators?

Bill managed to keep the engine running in spite of the abrupt halt. Our hearts were pounding louder than the pistons. The lions moved closer, in their time, elegant, leathal, undeterred and in control. They stalked the two beamed smoking intruder with the wet white human cargo. We sat in the dark knowing there was little to do except wait for their decision, hope, pray and sweat.

The lions looked us over, seemed unimpressed and left. Spam in a can, with petrol sauce on the side, was rejected. They moved out of our headlights and into the dark envelop of the Amboselli, after other fare. The queen of beasts vanished, off to work, off to beat the lame and the not so lame, off to dine, table for three, rare for all.

"William, any thought of pitching a tent and sleeping on the ground is ancient history. A fortress will be just fine."

The nearest fortress, the once vanishing lights of the Serena Lodge, finally reappeared. We drove toward the lights and eventually parked our truck in a walled compound. A life-long act of opening the door of a motor vehicle was now a new experience. Even though we were safely inside the lodge parking area, we looked fore and aft and looked again for any sign of animal before cautiously, ever so cautiously, opening the doors. Then and only then, on legs that were not altogether steady, we left the questionable safety of the truck. Under the bright flood lights of the Lodge we carried our gear to the entrance, swiveling our heads and looking in every direction along the way. Legs were not working the way legs should work. The lions, after all, were not in a zoo.

The Lodge receptionist confirmed that she did have beds and hot water and, yes, it was not too late for food if we hurried for the kitchen was about to close. Best of all, we learned there was a bar and we did not have to hurry. At that moment I had a clear understanding of the word "oasis."

The tension of the day was now telling. We were stiff and sore with plenty of aches from bouncing off the inside of the truck while negotiating endless ruts and bumps. The emotion and the tension of the trip in the dark through wildebeest, hyena, elephant and lion, straining to see the trail and locate the Lodge or a safe camp had created a major case of weary.

I signed the register for the team of two and the smiling native hostess handed me a key. It is a simple event, this passing of the key from innkeeper to tired traveler. As a business traveler, I participate in this ritual about thirty weeks of the year. But this check-in was a singular event. There was no American plastic key holder adorned with a gold stamped corporate logo proclaiming Marriott or Hyatt. The key, oh so most appropriate for this Kenyan venue, was attached to a very large bone.

The irony made me smile and I could not resist. Life does not present many opportunities this good to tweak a friend and administer a little practical joke. I gave the key back to the receptionist and announced, "William, I'll get the bags you take the key."

Bill walked over to the reception desk and extended his hand. The receptionist placed the bone in the palm of his hand with a light slap, as one would pass a baton. The startled Bill looked down and then up and then down again and quietly, while expelling air from his lungs, said, "Ohhhhhh no." He rolled his eyes and leaned against the reception desk, staring at the bone.

My skeletal training at this point in life consisted of two scrubs in surgery with orthopedic surgeon Dick Buechel and many in depth discussions with orthopedic surgeon Ephriam Wilkinson on the best way to butterfly a leg of lamb. Damned if I could identify the bone or the source. They, at very least, would have been creative schemers and made something up.

Bill, ever the student, looked at me, extended the bone and said, "Any ideas, big guy?"

"No, don't have a clue," I replied, "but it's a little short for a femur. It's probably from the last two guys who tried to drive across the Amboseli at night."

We both laughed. The receptionist laughed. But our laughs sounded a bit hollow.

Several bottles of cold Kenyan beer, appropriately named Tusker, eased our aches and pains. We replayed the day while sitting in an open air bar complete with thatched roof and overlooking a watering hole just yards away. A flood light played on the pond. The tall grass at the far edge and a small area of trampled mud indicated that animals did come to drink As we talked we watched the shadows on the other side of the water for any hint of movement. The night was dark and we still felt like the hunted.

There were two lasting images from an incredible day of adventure: the old man at Sultan Hamud, hunched over an ancient foot powered sewing machine, eye's dull with fatigue and lost interest; and, in the dark of the Amboseli, two red eyes, hungry red eyes, intent on a kill, watching four wide white eyes pass.

We would sleep. The red eyes would play the nightly drama of the African plain, the oldest theater in the world. Morning light would come and find new bones. Scavengers would then sweep the theater clean and the stage would be readied for the next performance.

"No, You May Not Cross The Border, It Is Too Much Trouble."

Namanga, Arusha, Moshi, and Marangu is not an African law firm. It is our route of travel and my turn to drive. I would pilot from the Amboseli and the key-bone hotel to the border crossing at Namanga, into Tanzania and on to the foot of Kilimanjaro.

We were up at day break and decided to back track in the direction of the elephant herd. We very much wanted to see the elephants in daylight and make some photographs.

The herd was just a few minutes away and we approached very slowly. Evidently they had worked their way toward the lodge during the night. There were thirty-two elephants, several young and a few bulls with enormous curved tusks, enough to make a poacher swoon.

As we watched the elephants in silence it was hard to believe the Kenyan elephant population, once numbering in the hundreds of thousands (one report indicated half a million) was now down to an estimated 20,000. Poachers were slaughtering elephants just for the tusks and selling the prized ivory in the international market. Poaching is illegal, however policing a range as big as Kenya is extremely difficult. Even though rangers are well armed and have shoot-to-kill orders poachers continue to slaughter elephants. Sadly enough, they cut out the valuable ivory tusks and leave hide and meat for scavengers.

"Take a long look William, you are watching the equivalent of a wild American buffalo herd. Soon this image may be history."

"Do rocks move?" Bill replied.

"I don't think we had that much beer last night."

"Then we have a very small elephant out there."

I attached a 200mm lens to my Nikon and began looking for the small elephant. And there it was, a small moving "rock" flanked by an ever vigilant mother elephant. It may have been four feet high, only a few weeks old, if that. Somehow I had never imagined wrapping my arms around an elephant. Giving a warm hug to a cat or dog, yes, but to an elephant? Not likely. But given a chance, that was the feeling I had watching the babiest of baby elephants.

God, it has been said, watches over drunks and little children. God must also watch over disoriented adventurers driving the Amboseli in the dark of the night. How we had managed to careen through this herd without bumping an elephant, particularly a baby, was almost beyond a question. How, indeed! Our unfortunate behavior must have been protected by luck, driving skill and divine intervention.

As I watched the elephants many emotions played in my head and heart. And then came the zap! The pow! of a distant memory. Synapses connected and crackled and the wheels of recall were spinning. I was now back in first grade at Franklin School on Bridge Street in Wausau, Wisconsin. It must have been 1947.

We were given mimeographed outlines of animals, a large number ten can of broken crayons and instructed to color the animals "carefully." It was a dark day when the teacher handed us the outline of an elephant. None of us had ever seen a real live elephant. Things began to go wrong when I found an almost intact orange Crayon. Clearly it was a whopper, the biggest in the can. We were all in the erroneous "bigger is better" mind set so I was delighted and began coloring the elephant using fast and loose strokes. In no time at all I had colored the elephant and, when I held it up for all to see, the roof fell in. The teacher pointed out, for all to hear, that I had committed multiple grievous errors. I had colored "outside the lines" and I had colored an elephant orange. "There are no orange elephants," said the teacher, bruising me for life.

Fast forward forty years. I'm standing on the soil of the Great Rift Valley in East Africa admiring a herd of real elephants. Through a telephoto lens I discover a baby elephant, just days old and less than one hundred yards away. Mother elephant is dusting the child with the reddish-brown soil of southern Kenya. There is red dust all over the place. Mother elephant is definitely coloring outside the lines. In the early morning sun of this glorious clear African day, the baby elephant looked . . . orange.

I emitted a muffled cheer, so as not to spook the elephants. I wanted to cheer loudly and jump into the air, raising my arms in triumph. Vindication! I was finally able to throw off first grade induced feelings of failure. Tough year that first grade.

Amazing recollection, I thought. The American education system works just fine if you conform and are average. If you conform you are rewarded with good grades. If you are an exception and you become creative and color outside the lines you are penalized. If you are gifted or on the other end of the spectrum and considered "slow" there isn't much for you except conflict. What perfect educational madness.

We reluctantly left the elephant herd and felt a tremendous sense of freedom as we drove in virtually any direction to move closer to a variety of game. In a matter of minutes we drove very close to zebra, cape buffalo, Thompson gazelle, giraffe, green monkeys and the ever present un-wieldy beast. After years of conditioning, driving only on marked roads and at a controlled speed, the ability to drive, at will, in any direction is hard to adjust to, but terrific when you arrive.

On the western edge of the Amboseli we approached another guard post with yet another flimsy stick of a barricade blocking the road. The guards lobbied successfully and we agreed to take an off-duty colleague to Namanga for what could be described as liberty. The smiling guard took his place on the back seat, centered himself and did not bother with the seat belt. Brave lad. I was driving.

We quickly learned that vehicles are scarce and far too expensive for a majority of natives. If you are fortunate enough to have a vehicle you are expected to fill any empty seats with Africans and provide neighborly transport.

The day was bright, the road was terrible and the best I could do was an aggressive 30 miles per hour. We bounced, we banged and rocked all the way to Namanga. Bill and I bitched and moaned all the way. The guard smiled.

Namanga—Definitely Not Our Kind Of Town

Namanga is an armed camp. The Kenyan border guards are separated from the Tanzanian border guards by a one hundred yard stretch of road lined with shacks offering food, drink and places to sleep . . . . all grim. Once you clear Kenyan customs to leave their country you must run the gauntlet and deal with Tanzanian customs agents to receive permission to enter their country. It is difficult to say which set of officials is more of a pain in the wallet. Their mission seems to be to make the border crossing as difficult as possible. We heard stories of two and three day delays in border crossings at Namanga.

It is clear the Kenyan guards and the Tanzanian guards do not like one another. The border between the countries had been closed for many years and only recently re-opened. The atmosphere was oppressive. Give an African official a rubber stamp, a little authority and a uniform and you have created a monster. Add a gate across the road and an automatic military weapon and you have squared the monster.

I approached the Kenyan guard, passport in hand and explained our purpose and our plan. He listened impatiently and glared. "Who said you could take that vehicle out of Kenya?" He spat the words with contempt.

Taking a deep breath, for he was in total control, I gently explained that it was a rented vehicle and we had decided to take the truck to Tanzania.

"You cannot! No! You must have permission. You must have form C-3 from the government transportation office in Nairobi. You must have log book from the Central Bank in Nairobi. It will take two, maybe three days. There is no other way."

Silence and disbelief from the Mages-Jackson expedition. He continued.

"The Tanzanians will want a vehicle fee. It is too much. No, you may not cross the border, it is too much trouble. There is nothing to do here. You cannot go in the Kenyan truck."

My initial reaction, while attempting to control my temper, was a sinking feeling in my stomach, and I really didn't like the feeling . . . much less the arrogant guard fueling it. A year of planning and the dream of climbing the highest mountain on the African continent were being dashed by the SOB (Sweet Old Borderguard).

Bill, who normally takes no prisoners, was also trying to control his temper. We bought time using the old "we didn't know that" routine of the fumbling, bumbling tourist.

The SOB held his ground. He was trying to intimidate us and had nearly succeeded. His argument made no sense. His smirking smile at our discomfort finally managed to illicit some good old American resistance.

It is damn tough to smile at someone, to control your tone of voice and appear reasonable when you really want to strangle them. We offered no bribe and he offered no solution. It was a classic standoff. I turned to Bill and my body language took the guard out of the picture.

"Well, William my friend," I began in a confident deductive tone, "we have no choice but to drive back to Nairobi, relate this man's refusal to let us cross the border, file a complaint with the government, alert the vehicle officials, turn in the car, go to the airport and fly to Tanzania."

"That's it," Bill replied, "we tell the government what happened here, drop the car and spend our dollars on airplane tickets. Do you think this guy will be in trouble?"

"I really don't know, but he's an important man and can probably handle it."

Silence from the important man in the guard uniform.

We turned and began to leave. I thought, I'll give him about five steps away and he'll cave.

At stride number four the guard said, "OK, you could try the Tanzanians, you could try. If they can decide something you can go. But I don't think it possible. There is nothing I can do. I am helpless." Then he fled and was replaced by another guard who stamped our passports with indifference disguised as ink.

With churning stomachs and growing anger we wondered what official Africa would provide on the Tanzanian side of the gauntlet.

I suggested that Bill stay with the truck while I walked the hundred yards to the Tanzanian border office to see if "something can be done." Our passports had been stamped but the truck was still in question. About half way down the road it occurred to me that the Tanzanians wouldn't know that. If we drove up to their office they might assume that all was well. I turned around and headed back, passing the dilapidated shops and dozens of black faces tracking my every step. I felt like an enemy intruder in no-man's land waiting for the first shot to be fired.

I joined Bill in the truck and told him the plan. We would drive off as if everything was A-OK and let the Tanzanians deal with two tourists eager to visit their country. We would also introduce some dollars into the process. I related an old axiom: money is like snow on the ground, it makes it easier to pull the sled. We were oh so close to our objective, time to experiment.

It is amazing how things began to move when we distributed American dollars. Barriers disappeared, restrictions began to crumble and guards became very passive.

One helpful official with a clipboard was dispatched to obtain our engine number, evidently an important paperwork item and a requirement for taking a Kenyan truck into his country. Bill and I searched the engine compartment from top to bottom scrapping away grease, dirt and oil trying to find the engine number. The number had to be stamped into the engine block somewhere. I crawled under the truck and had no luck.

The young official grew impatient and looked at an aluminum plate attached to the fire wall with small screws. The plate sported the Isuzu logo in color, with the name of the truck and the model number. He brushed it lightly with his hand, smiled, wrote down the model number, said "Good enough" and presented the form for our signature. We signed the bogus document and were stamped into Tanzania.

One hurdle remained, the guard house and gate. I drove forward, papers and passport in hand. A fatigue clad soldier with an automatic rifle did not bother with papers or passport, just looked at me with a hint of a friendly smile and asked if we would take a rider. We indicated we would rather not. The faint smile vanished and he indicated that if we didn't take the rider he was not going to open the gate. My smile now appeared and I indicated we would be more than happy to take a rider. All this indicating produced a well dressed Wachagga girl, perhaps 17 or 18. She beamed as she climbed into the back seat and waved at the guard. With a flourish he opened the gate and we were finished with Namanga. To say we were relieved is the very definition of understatement.

At Longido (no gas pump, no broken bus, no chickens, but one police hut) the girl motioned for us to stop, jumped out, beamed a smile, said, "asante sana," Swahili for many thanks, and she was gone.

With the native girl safely delivered to Longido our conversation quickly turned to Namanga, clearly not our kind of town. We knew Africa was poor, we expected poverty and we even concluded that Americans would be perceived as ugly prosperous Americans in this very different land. But the attitude of African officials was still very difficult to swallow. We concluded the official salute was an out-stretched hand, palm up.

It was also hard to forget the belligerent attitude of the Kenyan border official who was clearly trying to intimidate and work us for a bribe. His hostility and refusal to allow us to take our Kenyan truck out of Kenya, reciting a litany of what must have been creative restrictions, still burned. He began with an angry "You can't take that truck into Tanzania" then moved to "Nothing can be done" followed later by "See if the Tanzanians can decide something." In a schizophrenic twist, as he walked away in a huff, he smirked and said, "We try to be very nice to tourists."

As we drove through northern Tanzania we were impressed with the contrast. Kenya had been flat, bare and void of life and color. Flat and bare gave way to gently rolling hills, fields of corn and, as we reached Arusha and Mt. Meru, dark green coffee bushes and banana trees.

The Republic of Tanzania had once been Tanganyika and populated by Dutch and German farmers. An alliance in 1964 with the island sultanate of Zanzibar produced a new country with a new name. Tanzania appeared to embrace a socialist philosophy and many things seemed nationalized. Kenya is a pro-western nation but somehow Tanzania looked better to the avowed capitalist mountaineers looking for Mt. Kilimanjaro.

We passed through the towns of Arusha and Moshi during what we would call the evening rush hour. Driving on the left side of the road with the steering wheel on the right side of the truck still felt unusual on this second day of our trip. I had the pleasure of driving and dodging school children, herds of animals, potholes big enough to have names, many careening buses jam packed with passengers and goods, smoking trucks and swarms of natives on foot and bicycle.

Bill fidgeted and occasionally flinched in the passenger seat. The guy in left front seat has the worst deal. There are no shoulders on the few semi-paved roads and the passenger feels like he is coming very close to roadside stationary objects and not-so-stationary Africans. The constant bouncing and dodging causes nerve ends to crackle. At least the driver has a steering wheel to hang onto and usually knows where the truck will be aiming.

The road was a lane and a half wide. The driver, as a result, is cheek to cheek with passing vehicles on the right. The busses (chief form of native transportation) passing on the right were close enough to smell the humanity packed into and dangling out of them. It seems amusing now, but I recall the shock of watching a pair of native legs swinging out from the back of the bus toward our passing truck. A man was hanging onto an exterior luggage rack with both hands. As the bus bucked and weaved down the road his legs would swing from side to side. As we passed his feet swung out toward our windshield. I had never hit anyone in the feet with a windshield before. Somehow we missed.

To drunks, little children and errant adventurers we added airborne Africans. God, we concluded, must be a very busy guy.

At the village of Marangu we spotted a small sign for the Kibo Hotel. The road took us through a dark jungle of lush and green. After a few more bounces, bumps, twists and turns we arrived at the aging hotel and were greeted by two smiling native boys in what could pass for bellman jackets. "Jambo, jambo" (hello, hello) they shouted. We had arrived at the base of Mt. Kilimanjaro.

Mt. Kilimanjaro
Wednesday (continued)

A Snow Capped Mountain At The Equator?
Scientifically Impossible!

> *"I fancied I saw the summit . . . covered with*
> *a dazzling white cloud. My guide called*
> *the white which I saw merely 'beredi' or*
> *cold, but it was perfectly clear to me,*
> *however, that it could be nothing else but snow."*
>
> Johann Rebmann, 1848

A snow covered mountain at the equator? Impossible! So thought the great scientific minds of the day. The day was in the 19th Century—1848.

Johann Rebman, obviously a very determined and very brave German missionary, was the first European to see the mountain. He reported it to the European scientific and exploration communities. The scientific world was not prepared for his discovery. He was ridiculed in Europe. The Royal Geographic Society in England dismissed his observation as "figments of imagination . . . of reasonable evidence of perpetual snow there is not a tittle offered."

Rebmann's discovery was attacked with fierce criticism. Some even proved "scientifically" that snow at the equator was impossible. English geographer, William Cooley earned himself a place in history by calling the find a "fairy tale" and suggested that Rebmann should have his mind examined by a doctor.

It seems clear to me that part of the problem of acceptance rests with Rebmann's unfortunate choice of words. He was a brave explorer and a lousy writer. The word "fancied" was a popular term in his era and could be interpreted as "imagined."

A simple lack of knowledge among the Royal scientists in England was certainly the major problem. They had no understanding of the affect of altitude on temperature. And time after time they proved they were not futurists. For example, in the last days of the 19th Century Royal scientists were asked by the Crown for their assessment of the notion that heavier than air machines might actually fly. Came the report—no chance, impossible, forget it. A limited lot. Not surprising they had trouble with the pairing of snow and equatorial heat.

Fifteen years after Rebmann's discovery, while the American Civil War was raging, others confirmed that Kilmanjaro was not a figment of his imagination or a "fancy" of any kind. There, indeed, was a permanently snow capped mountain three degrees south of the equator. One hundred and fifty-five years later I can confirm that the snow is still there.

Mt. Kilimanjaro, known affectionately as "Kili" by those who climb it, is truly the undisputed king of African mountains. It rises sharply out of the East African Plateau to a height of 5,895 meters or 19,339 feet. While Kilimanjaro is a world class mountain it is also very unusual in that it is not part of a mountain chain. There are no foothills or other mountains leading up to Kili. There is nothing to obscure its breadth and height. It is one very large volcano sitting all by itself on a flat African plain. It's as if the great developer in the sky was going to create a mountain range, made one gigantic mountain to anchor the development, then became distracted and went off to pursue something else.

The condition that makes an ascent of Kilimanjaro special and difficult is the incredible altitude gain from the village of Marangu to the summit. The base of Kili at Marangu, where one begins the long climb to the summit, is under 6,000 feet, just slightly higher than Denver, Colorado. When (and if) you reach the summit at 19,339 you have experienced an altitude gain of more than 13,000 feet.

If you climb a typical 14,000 foot mountain in America (as big as they get in the 48 States), it is not uncommon to begin climbing from a base of 8,500 feet, which produces an altitude gain of only 5,500 feet.

I have heard experienced mountaineers describe Mt. Kilimanjaro as a nice "walk up." As I studied the mountain and listened to climbers who had been on the mountain I didn't believe it. Even though the main route up the mountain is mostly a difficult hike followed by a long and punishing scramble it can hardly be described as a "walk." The altitude gain is far too great.

Kili's altitude gain and its height have been a problem for many highly trained and well conditioned mountaineers and adventurers. Harold Lange, in his 1982 book *"Kilimanjaro,"* notes that many renowned mountaineers have gotten into trouble on this challenging mountain.

"Among those who have returned home after unsuccessful attempts were Sir Edmund Hillary, one of the first two people to reach the summit of Mt. Everest and the highly trained and very fit hero of the first Moon landing, Neil Armstrong."

Just the same, about 500 persistent and courageous mountain climbers, hikers and well conditioned tourists, do reach the summit each year.

Like all mountains there is more than one route to the summit. On Kili there are five acknowledged routes. Limiting the routes and the climbers is a wise conservation move. Nature, at high altitude, is at once very hearty and extremely fragile. A footprint in a meadow at high altitude might remain to disfigure the ground for many years. Plant growth that has taken years and years of struggle just to survive, much less thrive, could be crushed and destroyed forever in a single human step. That the Kenyans and Tanzanians are limiting climbers to a few restricted routes is most appropriate. Now, if they would only do more to protect the animals.

First On The Summit—Black Leopard Or German Geographer?

The first attempt to climb the snowcapped mountain, that European scientists insisted could not possibly exist, was made in 1861. The leaders of the expedition made an unfortunate decision and began climbing during the rainy season. They suffered greatly and were forced off the mountain at only 8,360 feet, more than 11,000 feet from the summit. Several in the party died.

Climbers continued to attempt the ascent, some reaching as high as 16,500 feet only to be repelled by exhaustion and exposure.

In 1887 and again in 1888 a Leipzig geographer, Hans Meyer tried to reach the summit and failed. There was charm in his third attempt. On October 6, 1889, at 10:30 AM, Meyer became the first human being to ever set foot on the summit of Mt. Kilimanjaro.

I had been fascinated with Kilimanjaro for years, long before I knew I would someday be committed to climb very high mountains on all seven continents. Mountaineering, I discovered and learned, is much more than a sport. It is an adventure, education, a personal challenge and a romance with rugged and often pristine beauty.

I can trace the seed of my fascination to Ernest Hemmingway's short story, *"The Snows Of Kilimanjaro."*

"Kilimanjaro is a snow covered mountain 19,710 feet high and is said to be the highest mountain in Africa. Its western summit is called by the Masai 'Ngaja Ngai,' the House of God. Close to the summit there is the dried frozen carcass of a leopard. No one has explained what the leopard was seeking at that altitude."

And what would we be seeking at that altitude? Adventure? Certainly. But the climb would also be a test of will, of stamina, of courage and judgment. It would also be a search for beauty, the raw beauty of the mountain and the fragile beauty of the human soul. With the physical challenge would go the ever present hope that this amazing experience would result in some degree of personal growth.

Unlike the leopard, I knew we would have the discipline and the good sense to come down if we sensed serious respiratory or neurological problems associated with high altitude, a lack of oxygen and the accompanying stress.

Mountains are very unforgiving. There is considerable danger on any big mountain. Weather will kill you before the classic or well recorded fall. Bad judgment, however, is the most lethal foe. As altitude robs the brain of oxygen, altitude sickness in many forms will occur. Every climber will experience it. To persist and continue to climb to the summit, in spite of the complications of altitude sickness, takes a great deal of self-discipline. Making the summit often depends less on muscle and more on self-motivation. More than once I wondered, with a bow to author Tom Wolfe, if we would have "the right stuff."

We would go up the mountain. How high would be anyone's guess. We would assume the risk. We would accept whatever the mountain delivered. By placing ourselves in the path of danger we would enjoy the growth that comes from exceeding the comfortable and the safe; the growth that comes from finding out you can endure more than you ever imagined.

We were prepared to climb to the top of Mt. Kilimanjaro, the highest mountain in Africa, with more confidence than fear and with a healthy respect for the mountain, to see if the leopard was still there.

The Kibo Hotel—Provisions, Porters And Pilsner

The once grand Kibo Hotel was old and worn, but the gardner (bless him) was still doing his best. The grounds in the wet-green jungle clearing supported many healthy rose bushes and large hibiscus.

The two story Kibo was built by German settlers in the colonial days. The Germans were gone and with them the order and care that made the Kibo a legendary shelter at the base of Kilimanjaro.

We checked in and as I carried my gear up the dark wooden staircase it became 1945. The carpet runner on the stairs and in the halls looked like something from my grandmother's house. It was faded and worn. Everything was darkly stained and dimly lit. Our room smelled like a musty old cabin in the woods that had not been opened in several seasons. Grateful to be out of our bouncing truck I stretched out on one of the metal framed beds only to discover it was very friendly. It literally wrapped around my weary body with a mild and musical protest. The springs had long since retired preferring to embrace rather than support. One day, I mused, I'll become a spring.

My nap was interrupted by a call to dinner. I splashed some cold water on my face (no hot water in evidence) and descended to the dining room. It was a classic high ceiling dining hall supported by large wooden pillars. The walls were covered with banners, pictures, and posters inscribed by various climbing teams that had used the Kibo as base camp. Most, I noted, had made it up and down the mountain successfully. Climbers from thirty countries were represented on the peeling walls of the Kibo.

The Kibo kitchen proved once more that one does not go to Africa for the food. It was plain and unremarkable. Dessert was fruit cocktail directly from the can, and I did not get the lone cherry.

Native hotel workers wore light blue jackets which were clean but as worn and patched as the hotel. The jackets were starched and pressed and manners were evident, suggesting some formal training had taken place. We were told that a German widow had owned and operated the hotel until her recent death. The service at the Kibo reflected her influence—definite tones of European quality.

Although not advertised, there was a bar with a simple back bar of wooden shelves, and a sparse collection of spirits (I recognized not one label). There was also a treasure chest. Behind the bar stood a dark wooden ice box with a glass window. The window had the unmistakable condensation that promised cold beer. Within were several bottles of Tanzanian pilsner which we liberated.

During dinner we had been informed that the hotel manager would brief us on the climb and help us with provisions. We joined him in his office and it was clear from his facial expression, tone of voice and body language he was not in love with tourists. He was cool and almost dictatorial. While he was not in uniform, I did search his office for rubber stamps and automatic rifles.

His attitude inferred that we were being granted a privilege. I wasn't sure whether the privilege was an audience with this self-important manager or the climb of Kilimanjaro. While climbing Kili does fall into the privilege category, we were also customers.

The manager detailed the number of guides and porters we would be taking, did a run down of necessary equipment and presented a cost which (no surprise) greatly exceeded our expectations. He fully appreciated that we were at his mercy and he would take no prisoners. After some debate in which we expressed our surprise at the cost he did offer a useful suggestion: we could climb alone or we could take other climbers with us to reduce the per person cost. Apparently solo climbers from all over the globe frequently gather at the Kibo to form a group and pool resources.

Bill and I had planned to do the climb alone so we gave him a "we'll think about it" reply. He shrugged his shoulders giving us a look that said, "I can get you now or get you later, it's all the same to me."

The supply room of the Kibo smelled of mothballs, oil and a hint of kerosene. It reminded me very much of a U. S. Army supply room. Olive drab materials were stacked with military precision—tents, rain flies, boots, wool shirts, parkas, walking sticks, railroad lanterns and other expedition items. We selected the only equipment we had not transported to Africa—large down-filled parkas suitable for an arctic winter. In the heat and humidity of the jungle the parkas, with their fur lined hoods, seemed the very definition of incongruity. But at the top, if we were lucky enough to make it to the summit, it would be bitter cold, below freezing and possibly below zero.

While provisioning for the climb it occurred to me that Kilimanjaro is unusual in many ways. For example, it would be possible to die of heat exhaustion at the base of the mountain or freeze to death at the top. To date, no one has managed to do both.

The young native store room clerk recommended an iron tipped walking stick. Normally I prefer both hands free when going up a mountain, unless an ice axe is required. Many climbers prefer a ski pole, a walking stick or something in hand for support. With the understanding that the receiver of communication must hear what is implied in a message as well as what is said, I decided the native clerk was offering advice as well as a walking stick. If nothing else, I thought, I can use the stick to beat off the psychic mountain gremlins that can sneak up behind a climber and sap or steal quarts of resolve or persistence. Although no one has ever seen one, I know they exist.

We poked through the collection of hiking sticks with the same care one uses when selecting the right golf club. Golf is a diabolical game in which you pay good money to take as few strokes as possible, when the pleasure of the game is hitting the ball. Go figure. Thinking of the steep course ahead I selected a double one iron and promised to keep my head down. I was secretly delighted that the wooden sticks were tipped with iron. I have never been able to successfully hit a wood on any golf course. Wood, I concluded long ago, is best used for starting fires.

Although we had transported vital gear to Africa—dome tents, inflatable moisture barriers, down-filled sleeping bags, and sturdy mountain boots—we discovered it is quite possible to completely outfit a climb in the Kibo Hotel supply room.

At the suggestion of His Honor the manager, we met two travelers who wished to climb Kili and share the expense. We did so a bit reluctantly, for Bill and I knew and trusted one another, knew our physical and mental limits and our athletic ability. Accepting two total strangers with unknown climbing experience was a risk.

We could not have been more fortunate. David Schrock and Frankie Spite were not only superb personalities, but David had more mountaineering experience than Bill and Pat. Both David, a 30ish Irishman living in America, and Frankie, a twenty-something New Zealand lady, working her way around the world, had far more international travel experience. We happily agreed to do the mountain together.

After one Tanzanian brandy, masquerading as cognac, we retired to our room, took our last showers (no hot water) and then tossed and turned on sagging beds through the night, which included a heavy rain storm. Wonderful, I thought, the footing in the jungle would be grease over tree roots. A shame to lose the mountain over a sprained or broken ankle while working through the jungle at the base of the mountain.

Bill and I both snore, although noble confessions being good for the soul, he is the weaker of the two by far. Although I try to minimize the noise by sleeping on my side, invariably I roll over in the night and the decibel level increases greatly. Bill, on this subject, is a veteran. He described, in his been there-done that style, that his dad rivaled my performance. As a kid, he and his brother would simply shout, "Hey, dad, roll over." His father would wake up, roll on his side and the Jackson brothers would go back to sleep. It was a simple system that worked, until dad rolled on his back again and they repeated the command. Bill now uses the same system on me.

Sleep came in spurts. We were both excited. I had been dreaming of this climb for a long time and had examined African maps for many hours trying to imagine what life would be like in this part of the world. I had traced the routes up Kili many, many times. The map was now reality. We would actually begin climbing one of the world's most impressive mountains in a few hours.

Beginning The Ascent Of Kili—4,500 feet to 8,800 feet

The day was misty, overcast and warm in the rain forest at the base of the mountain. I leaned against the rough plaster wall on a crude second story balconey overlooking the entrance to the Kibo Hotel. The roses and hibiscus, which were impressive the day before, were even more beautiful in the soft morning light. Their colors, a variety of reds and yellows, were in sharp contrast to the wet sea of green surrounding the hotel. There were no butterflies darting about the flowers. The butterflies had collected en mass and decided to bounce around the walls of my stomach. We met David and Frankie, who looked eager and well rested.

David was lean and fit, suitable for an assistant track coach at San Jose State in California. Between terms at San Jose, David worked as a tour bus driver in Europe and Asia and had spent considerable time in India and Nepal. Frankie was a physical therapist who actually listed her occupation as "traveler." She would travel as far as she could, obtain a job, work as long as local government regulations allowed and then travel to the next country and engage in the next adventure. When she could not find work as a therapist she waited tables and tended bar to make ends meet. Judging from what she said, ends rarely met in her lifestyle.

David smiled a warm greeting and indicated that we had an opportunity to add additional climbers to the party. Each climber we added would spread the cost. He made a strong argument for cost reduction, since he and Frankie were on a very limited budget. So, we agreed to meet with the candidates.

A bespectacled Bruno Schmidt was a young German chemical lab assistant. He lived in Munich, spoke limited English, limited Swahili and excellent German. He reported extensive mountain climbing experience in the European Alps and was traveling Africa alone with little more than a backpack and a passport.

The second candidate was an American, Dwight Plunkett, a white collar computer rep from Houston. He was tall, lanky and self-assured. His manner was so quiet it made you question whether he was a real Texan. Dwight's hobby was outdoor adventure and he had chosen well. He, too, was traveling alone.

Bill, David, Frankie and I huddled to decide whether to include Bruno and Dwight. I knew Bill would have trouble with anything German. His dad had been a naval officer and memories of World War II die hard. Bruno, although not born until well after the war, could hardly be held responsible for German atrocities. I was a bit surprised when Bill cast a vote, however reluctant, to admit the German and the Texan.

The make-up of our team was set and took on a distinct United Nations flavor. The climbers would be David Shrock, Ireland; Frankie Spite, New Zealand; Bruno Schmidt, Germany; Mages and Jackson representing the United States, and Dwight representing Texas . . . five countries in total.

The Kibo manager, introduced us to our guides and assistant guides, both Wachagga natives with years of experience climbing Kili. If it isn't rule one in mountaineering it should be; always climb with a local guide. In Africa native guides and porters are relatively inexpensive. It makes no sense to do without. Our native team would consist of a guide, two assistant guides and six or seven porters, who would carry all our gear. Having climbed extensively in the States, where you carry your own gear in a heavy back pack, this was luxury of the first order.

Our chief guide was Felix Ansa Ocotu. Felix, about 35 years old, possessed the sterling qualities of a successful guide. He was patient, friendly, and very confident. His second in command was a 27 year old Tanzanian who had grown up as an orphan and raised by the nuns at the local mission. They had named him Goodluck Christopher.

The other natives on the team kept a distance from us and we did not get to know them very well. The porters ranged in age from very young to very old. The distribution of porter assignments clearly involved the entire community.

We were introduced to the porters and they gathered around our group, shook hands and provided friendly greetings in a mixture of Swahili and English. Most of them offered warm, genuine smiles of welcome.

The prevailing attitude in our group, which we very much wanted to project, was that we viewed ourselves as guests in their neighborhood. We returned the smiles and did our best to communicate a sense of respect for the porters and guides. I had read stories of conflict between natives and climbers, mostly based on the superior attitude or racial prejudice of the white-faced climbers. I was personally determined there would be none of that on our ascent of Kili and I made it my mission to monitor the relationship between native and climber. We would show them the respect they deserved and we would treat them as members of the team.

As we milled about outside the Kibo I noted that all the members of our climbing group were under 30, except Bill who was 32. At 45 I was the old guy. I do not consider myself old, in any sense. Old, like the psyche of Ireland, is a state of mind, not an age. I recalled jazz singer Mel Torme's arrangement of "You Make Me Feel So Young" in which he sings the verse: "Unless your head is made of lumber, you know that age is just a number . . . "

The oldest porter in the group, William, stood next to me and said, "All are younger. You are the elder." He smiled a good-natured smile. I sensed from the grey in his hair he was in his late 50's, perhaps older. I slowly linked my arm in his, while the other porters looked on, and I spoke directly to him.

"Mr. William, since you and I are older and wiser than this group of young goats, we shall have to do our best to keep them out of trouble on Kili."

There was immediate laughter from some of the porters who understood English. Translations to Swahili happened very quickly and soon all the porters were smiling and laughing. William beamed and proudly squeezed my arm. He had broken the ice and I had signaled the porters, one and all, that we were worthy of their friendship.

On that high note, we all piled onto the back of a pick up truck which would carry us to the trail head. The truck swerved and bounced through the jungle, with one stop for fresh meat and other provisions.

The supermarket was a simple lean-to in a clearing, an open air butcher shop. A cow had been slaughtered and a large native woman with a very big knife was quickly separating skin and bone with some experienced whacks and chops. We were, I assumed, looking at tonight's supper. As an enthusiastic amateur chef I wondered about the cut we would see at camp number one and how it might be prepared.

The scene had an ancient quality to it. The white skin of the cow looked like chalk against the deep green of the wet forest. Children and neighbors ringed the clearing cheering the butcher on. The event was as much entertainment and contest in this quiet jungle as it was commerce. Her heavy arm moved up and down with force and purpose, the knife slashed the air. She was making quite an impression. The cow was not faring well.

Once cut, a large chunk of meat disappeared into a woven sack and our truck rolled on.

Kilimanjaro is a national park and is tightly controlled by the government. Well, as tight as it gets in Africa. This should, I thought, prevent developers from creating condos and theme parks. The very idea sent shivers down my spine. Who in their right mind would desecrate this incredible mountain with commercial this and that? And the other voice in my head said, "Hell, only millions of business people who don't give a damn about preserving natural beauty."

At the park gate we checked in and obtained permits to enter the park and climb the mountain. For those uninitiated in the mountaineering world, most world mountains are in parks or preserves and require a fee and a permit. The Tanzanian fee for Kilimanjaro was $140 per climber. Ever the critic, Bill quickly pointed out that a year long pass to American national parks could be had for much less. We contrasted the two figures with the Nepal government charge for a Mt. Everest expedition permit (over a hundred thousand dollars) and decided we had a definite bargain.

The Kilimanjaro trail head at the park gate is high above the Kibo Hotel at 6002 feet. The Kibo is at 4500 feet. The truck had made the first 1500 feet of travel swift and pleasant. We would now begin the long slow trek to the top of the highest mountain in Africa. It would be long and slow, slow and long, with the emphasis on slow. A slow ascent makes perfect sense for it allows the body and the blood to adjust to diminishing levels of oxygen. Racing toward the summit, on the other hand, prevents acclimatization and often results in failure. We would go slow.

Passing Through Six Climate Zones

Our journey up Kilimanjaro would take us through six of the world's climate zones in three or four days, a very unusual passage.

We began in a rain forest at 5,940 feet. Our climb would take us through a cloud forest, a lower alpine meadow, an upper alpine meadow and a cold desert at 14,500 feet. We would rest in the cold desert before beginning the final ascent through permafrost, a frozen moonscape, at 18,000 feet and above. If we allowed our bodies and minds to adjust to a progressive lack of oxygen and significant changes in weather, we would reach the summit.

Camp One—Mandara Hut

Our plan was to ascend the mountain slowly and spend the night at three camps in three days. This is a rather typical approach to ascending a big mountain. Doing it in stages allows for the all important acclimitzation. Our first camp, Mandara, would be at approximately 9,000 feet.

The first day of the climb was a pleasant five hour hike through the rain forest. The jungle, as I expected, was wet steamy, muddy and very slippery. A light drizzle fell on and off all day and the footing was a challenge. Often the trail would become a mass of exposed tree roots and nimble became the order of the day. The picture was exactly what I imagined an African jungle to look like. Imagination and reality are seldom the same. This day they were.

We began the Kilimanjaro climb in very light clothing, shorts, t-shirts and running shoes. The running shoes were more comfortable at this low altitude than heavy mountain boots. We knew whatever we wore on our feet would become wet and soggy. We also knew that soggy mountain boots would not dry out and we would need them later on the final ascent, when the going gets really tough. So we correctly protected our boots, kept them dry and sloshed ahead in soaked running shoes.

The pace was steady and easy. Except for occasional chatter it was quiet and peaceful. Everyone seemed to be pre-occupied with personal thoughts. I found myself contrasting the cotton fields and open pastureland of west Tennessee, near my current home in Memphis, with the dark green dense tangle of an African rain forest. Quite a contrast.

We paused every hour or so to rest, sip some water, peel an orange or snack on a private reserve of candy. Then it was press-on, press-on, slow and easy does it, let the body adjust.

Ever alert for African wild life, we saw little except birds. This made sense, since our porters had been hiking ahead of us, transporting our gear and clearing the path in the process. The sound and scent of human animals passing through the forest scattered anything wild. I had mixed emotions. Safer to clear them out, infinitely more interesting to see them.

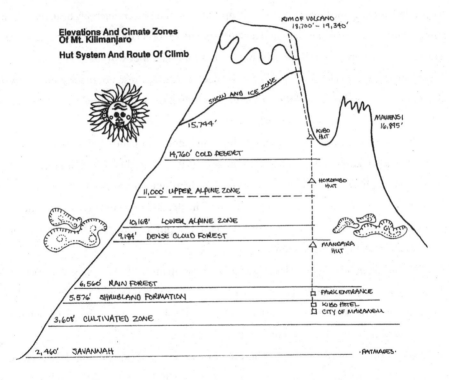

Elevations And Climate Zones Of Mt. Kilimanjaro

Hut System And Route Of Climb

RIM OF VOLCANO
18,700' – 19,340'

SNOW AND ICE ZONE

15,744'

MAWENSI
16,895'

KIBO HUT

14,760' COLD DESERT

11,000' UPPER ALPINE ZONE

HOROMBO HUT

10,168' LOWER ALPINE ZONE

9,184' DENSE CLOUD FOREST

MANDARA HUT

6,560' RAIN FOREST

5,576' SHRUBLAND FORMATION

PARK ENTRANCE
KIBO HOTEL
CITY OF MARANGU

3,608' CULTIVATED ZONE

2,460'   SAVANNAH

·PATMAGES·

We continued on, one foot ahead of the other, bobbing over slippery tree roots, weaving through vines and huge leafy plants, slowly gaining altitude and slowly dispersing the butterflies that had congregated in my stomach. Kilimanjaro was under foot . . . . and very much over head.

Late in the day we reached the first camp, Mandara Hut. I was prepared to sleep on the ground. I certainly didn't expect the wooden A-frame huts which explained the name of the camp. Wooden A-frame shelters were the contribution of the Norwegian Mountaineering Society, a superb volunteer effort. The floors of the huts were constructed about two feet off the ground, moving the body away from damp, cold soil and preserving body heat. Staying dry is important and even high tech mountain tents sometimes don't do the trick. The Norwegians had presented a very practical gift. The huts were simple and they worked.

Mandara Hut is a clearing at the top most edge of the rain forest. For the first time we were able to look up the shoulder of the mountain. I expected to be able to finally see the summit. All we could see was meadow and more meadow.

The porters had arrived at Mandara Hut long before our band of climbers, which says something about home field advantage. Acclimated as they were, they were able to travel faster even toting our heavy packs When we arrived they distributed our packs, matching gear with climber. So, we stripped off wet clothing, donned the dry and prepared bed rolls on the floor of the hut. A hut sleeps three. Bruno of Germany, Dwight of Texas and the author bunked together and waited the call to dinner.

This mountaineering experience was a first in so many ways. We enjoyed a reasonable shelter, a guide, assistant guide, a porter to carry the heavy stuff and a cook to prepare real food. I'm accustomed to a small tent or less, a 50 to 60 pound back pack on my aching back and freeze dried food, which only resembles real food.

I was certainly aware of the accouterments of some major expeditions and the culinary efforts made to prepare great food. I smile when I recall the account of an Italian team at base camp in Alaska on a Mt. McKinley glacier. They actually cracked real eggs, added extra virgin olive oil, mixed in hard Durham flour and rolled out fresh pasta. Now that's an expedition.

In 1880, not many years after mountaineering actually got its start in Chamonix, France, American author Samuel Clemens, Mark Twain's alter ego, spoofed the entire expedition idea in his fictional account of "The Ascent Of The Rifleberg." In his piece he detailed the make-up of a rather grand organization.

"The expedition," wrote Clemens, "consisted of 198 persons, including the mules; or 205 including the cows." The table of organization included the following:

Chiefs Of Service	Subordinates
Myself	1 Veterinary Surgeon
Mr. Harris	1 butler
17 guides	12 waiters
4 surgeons	1 footman
1 geologist	1 barber
1 botanist	1 head cook
3 chaplains	9 assistants
2 draftsmen	4 pastry cooks
15 barkeepers	1 confectionary artist
1 Latinist	

Over the years I have sent copies of this marvelous satire to many friends for I've never read anything as humorous about mountaineering. Every now and then someone would write back and ask, "So, how many do you take?" I always reported that I take myself, wear all hats and have great difficulty keeping a journal in Latin.

I found more than a little satisfaction in realizing I would now be able to report taking guides, assistant guides, porters and a cook.

The six from five countries gathered for the evening meal. Naturally we were curious. What had the chef prepared?

Felix, chief guide and now chief waiter, appeared with the feast. Over a wood fire the cook had prepared cabbage, potatoes and liver—thick slices of beef liver.

Liver is an either/or meat. You either love it or you despise it. There is no middle ground with liver. Personally, I love it, however it must be prepared very carefully. Many moms are probably responsible for developing liver haters. Their notion of cooking liver was to dredge it in flour and fry the living hell out of it till it was absolutely, positively dead. This produced a rubbery texture with a pasty flour coating along the edges. It also produced a strong gamey flavor many (myself included) found offensive.

Liver must be thick, well trimmed, sautéed in clarified butter to medium rare, and not beyond, then finished with sautéed onions a splash of good red wine, a touch of thyme (preferably fresh, not dried), and a generous dusting of fresh ground pepper. When served it should be topped with many slices of crisp smoked bacon, preferably apple wood smoked bacon from Neuske's in Wittenberg, Wisconsin. The best.

Our Tanzanian chef had no red wine. Onion was noticeably absent. I'm convinced bacon does not exist outside the Norfolk Hotel in Nairobi. And the liver had been roasted over a wood fire and tasted like wood. It was awful.

Our Irish friend, David Shrock had seconds, perhaps thirds.

We learned during the course of the journey that David had many endearing qualities that would cause you to trust him and follow him anywhere. Culinary taste was not one of them. If it is edible David will go for it. So, I quickly resolved not to follow him into restaurants, a resolution I willingly recanted at least twice later in the journey.

Following the dinner (cabbage and potatoes for me) we did what mountaineers so often do, sit in the dark and trade stories. The fine art of conversation and story telling are endangered ideas in a society where people expect to be entertained. But everyone in our camp eventually had something of interest to contribute and they told their stories with different styles. David proved to be a very good story teller bringing out the tension of adventure travel and sprinkling the incidents with humor. Bill did pointed commentary and critique, drawing from his endless reserve of fact, semi-fact, opinion and outrageous fiction. There are moments when he bests good stand up comedians with biting rants.

In the story telling department I can certainly hold my own, owing to significant Welsh blood. My grandfather was born and raised in Swansea, Wales. Admittedly, like good story tellers the world over, I never allow a fact to get in the way of a good yarn. Noble confessions being good for the soul, I do have a tendency to describe the building of a time piece instead of telling someone the time. But the connection of fly wheels and main springs is so very, very fascinating. Not so?

One of our porters suddenly materialized out of the dark. We never heard him coming. In the soft voice of the Wachagga, he asked in simple English if anyone would like to purchase a beer.

Time out! Purchase a beer? Purchase a beer on a mountain? On a mountain one only dreams of beer.

If this is a cruel joke, I thought, there would be roast porter the next night.

David turned and said, "Can you believe it mates, the lad has beer."

The enterprising porter decided a wooden beer case would balance on the head as well as anything else. He further deducted, with laser-like precision, that rookie Kili climbers would lust for a beer at the first camp. So, he carried a case of Tanzanian pilsner to Mandara Hut and jacked the price to match our altitude of 8,800 feet. We quickly peeled off the necessary shillings and procured twelve bottles of beer. We also tipped him well and he made a killing without lifting a spear.

As we sat in the dark, drinking beer and telling even better stories, I knew that somewhere Sam Clemens would be puffing a big fat cigar, smiling and making notes like crazy.

It was dark, but spirits were bright and getting brighter. Bill kept things rolling, punctuating his stories with unlimited facts and statistics about almost everything, including who was red-shirted in football at UCLA in 1982. I refer to it as his terabyte mode.

David related tour experiences. The span of subjects involved driving a huge Bedford truck with twenty British tourists through India and Nepal. Only Frankie and Bruno remained quiet. Bruno was unsure of his English and Frankie preferred to listen, observe and size up the group. A wise New Zealand lady. I attempted to involve her in the conversation.

"Frankie, America has developed a taste for your fish."

"Really, which fish is it?"

"Orange ruffy. It outsells almost everything at my market except salmon and cat fish. It is really quite good."

"Really?" She paused. "We throw it away."

Following her response it was very clear that our group knew how to laugh.

I crawled into my Blue Kazoo sleeping bag on the floor of the A-frame shelter. The bag was like an old friend and had protected me from the night air on many mountains. I found the wool navy watch cap I keep tucked in the bag and pulled it over my ears. The bag is an effective cocoon and the cap takes care of the balding head. At this point, I'd slept on mountains in Colorado, California, Washington, Oregon, Ireland and Scotland and had always been comfortable, even in the toughest weather. I shivered a bit thinking about Hans Meyer, the first to climb Kili in the 19th Century. No doubt, he slept in the open with minimal protection. Not surprising that some in his party died on the mountain.

The wooden planks of the hut were hard, but it was dry and dark and sleep came quickly.

Sleeping at altitude in thin air dreams seem more vivid. Over dinner one evening in the high Sierra of California, while visiting my friends Carol and Jim Carman in their mountain home, we all commented on the distinctive quality of dreams in the mountains. The next morning Carol inquired as to the quality of my dreams.

"Well, Carol, I dreamed I met soon-to-be Supreme Court Justice David Souter at a cocktail party."

"And how did you find him?"

"Oh, I found him to be extremely bright, very deep and most articulate. He is a good listener, definitely supports individual freedoms and I think will do his best to keep government at heel. From what he told me, I believe he will make a fine Supreme Court justice."

"Wonderful," she replied with a smile and offered me fresh raisin toast without batting an eye.

Everything seems so clear in mountain dreams. Perhaps we should move Congress into the mountains.

I'm very grateful for dreams. Dreams are the stuff of anything-and-everything-is-possible, the stuff of Walter Mitty. I'm also grateful for James Thurber who taught us the pleasure of retreating into dreams and becoming people we never were. I dreamed a Thurberesque dream at Mandar Hut.

I was with Ernest Hemingway in a camp on the Serengetti. We were in view of the dome of Kilimanjaro and well into a bottle of twelve year old single malt scotch. It was hot and he was ordering me to go up the mountain. I agreed and told him I wanted to find his leopard. With no trace of a smile, he told me that the leopard was the stuff writer's write and perhaps I should stay in camp and do the civilized thing—drink more scotch, which is the stuff good writer's drink. He intimated that the leopard just might have been a figment of the Great Ernesto's imagination; then again, he suggested it might not. With that pronouncement he had covered himself for all events. Should there be a leopard at the summit he would add to the Hemingway legend, which mostly existed in his own mind. Should there be no leopard at the summit of Kilimanjaro, then he would take credit for superior creativity, another legend in his own mind.

I spent the next several hours in the dream trying to walk up the side of the mountain without spilling my scotch. Two steps up and a slip down, then two more up and another slip down, cursing all the way. Over my shoulder, seated in his camp chair Hemingway appeared intense. His ample brow was furrowed, his bush shirt stained from the sweat of exertion. He wore a determined almost combative expression, as if he, not me, were struggling to climb the great mountain. He would later write, with full unearned first person flourishes, that *he* did ascend the mountain. I didn't even receive honorable mention.

This is the classic dream theme, a struggle to get somewhere one never ever gets. When I returned to my camp chair, soaked with sweat and exhausted, he clasped me on the shoulder and ordered me to make another attempt at the summit. He pushed me toward the mountain, pleased that I would try again, do the important work for him and stay the hell away from his scotch.

Mandara Hut to Horombo Hut—8,800 to 12,300 Feet

The gentle thumping on the door of the hut was our wake-up call. Felix The Concierge was on the job. From my vantage point on the floor I could see sky through a crack in the door. The weather looked promising. We were on the upper edge of the rain forest and about to break through the clouds that cling to the mountain more than 300 days of the year.

I sat up and leaned against the wall waiting for sleep to clear out and conscious to kick in. How ironic, I thought, to dream about Hemingway. 'Gotta love the mind and the way it works. I shook my head and smiled. Truly amazing.

The big oaf wanted me to do the heavy lifting so he could write the story. A definite con job. Papa Hemingway was a character. His life, I felt, was far more interesting than most of his novels. I had made this point in a college English paper and roundly pissed off the professor, who was a big time Ernesto fan. 'Curious that my bookshelf contains at least three biographies of the Oak Park, Illinois writer, including the classic by Carlos Baker. 'Curious that my book shelf contains only one collection of Hemingway short stories and none of his novels. Point made.

I stumbled out of the hut and made "hellos" and "good mornings" to one and all. Everyone seemed in good spirits, including Bill, who was doing "jambo, jambo" in an effort to go native.

Hot tea was served. Granted, it tasted like wood smoke, but then everything tasted like wood smoke. The tea was hot and strong and in a real ceramic mug. I cradled it in my hands, relished the warmth and then pressed it against my cheeks and forehead and shivered. The morning air at 8,800 feet was cool and damp.

Each morning began with hot tea and each day ended with hot tea. It was a ritual and the cook never missed. Tea and fruit became my staples.

Morning in the mountains requires an important decision—what to wear? The decision has little to do with appearance and everything to do with comfort and survival. Job one in mountaineering is to put one foot ahead of the other, safely and with persistence. What you wear can help your endurance or deplete it. Weather, heat loss, or over heating have probably caused more failed mountain ascents than the degree of the slope or the altitude. It is important to select the best layers of clothing for the day. It is a mix and match issue that has nothing to do with color.

We began the climb in the heat and mist of the rain forest. We wore light clothing that would wick away moisture. On this day we would emerge from the upper edge of the rain forest, work our way through a cloud forest and reach an alpine meadow. The day would require a bit more clothing. We opted to stay with wet running shoes and continue to keep our heavy boots dry for the final ascent.

One of the pleasures of mountain climbing, when you shed daily habits, is the almost complete disregard for non-essential grooming. What a pleasure not to shave. There are no mirrors . . . . none. Appearance does not matter. Run your fingers through your hair, brush your teeth, pull on a hat of some type and you are ready to go.

I've been with some first time hikers and climbers who insist on bringing the bathroom along. They even douse themselves with after shave lotion and effectively pollute the freshness of the mountain air.

I once went up a mountain with someone who actually brought along a compact hair dryer, the kind you plug in. When I saw it in his pack I was too embarrassed for him to even inquire. What on earth was he thinking? It was his one and only climb with us.

David Shrock won the prize for consistent AM enthusiasm. David greeted us each morning with an infectious smile and his Irish/American accent.

"Good morning mate, sleep well now, did you? It looks good this morning, wouldn't you say? You're looking chipper lad."

David is difficult to punctuate. His statements begin as statements and end up as questions. But he is always upbeat and positive.

The cook produced hot porridge. It tasted a lot like old fashioned library paste. Don't ask me how I know. I did the tea and oranges.

The final task in the morning is the packing of gear. Each climber is allowed about 20 pounds of gear. Each porter toted about 40 pounds on his head, so we buddied up and packed together. Bill and I shared one duffle. Joseph, our porter this morning, would hoist our load into the air, set it on his head, shake once or twice to center the load, find a balance point, and he was off and up the mountain. There have been attempts to introduce the native porters to conventional back packs. In one instance the back packs were explained and demonstrated, but quick as a flash, the natives removed the packs and put them on their heads.

On the trail I passed a porter from another team carrying a wooden crate on his head. "Ouch" was the only word that came to mind. Our porters, I duly noted, placed our duffle in a large plastic bag, sealed the bag and then put the plastic bag into a fiber gunny sack. Once secured it was water tight and softer on the old skull. We definitely had the smarter porters.

Our destination this day was Horombo Hut. We would be on the trail, climbing slowly, for six to seven hours. It appeared we would cover about 18 kilometers, almost eleven miles, and would move steadily upward from 8,800 to 12,300 feet, more than two miles above sea level.

As we moved up the mountain we encountered what appeared to be heavy, wet fog. The "weather" was actually a cloud bank. We had entered a cloud forest at 9,200 feet.

Kili, as we found on our drive through the Amboseli, is hard to detect even though there are no foothills and it is the only big mountain in the area. The mountain creates a semi-permanent ring of clouds and wears this collar beginning at about 9,200 feet and extending to about 10,500 feet. It is so persistent that the snow capped dome of Kilimanjaro is only visible a few days each year. This layer has earned the unusual designation as "cloud forest." I had never been on a mountain with a cloud forest, much less in one.

Plant life in the cloud forest was similar to the rain forest, but not quite as dense. The plants and the trees seemed to be getting along just fine with a maximum of cool moisture and a minimum of sunshine. Were I to live in a cloud forest I would soon resemble a shriveled prune, a very white shriveled prune.

In a few hours we broke out of the cloud layer and continued our slow pace into a high meadow. We were now in brighter light and open space and could see for miles.

Once in the clear everyone began to search for the summit, but it was not in sight. Vegetation began to thin, plants became smaller, bushes and clumps of elephant grass were seldom more than knee high. The altitude and lack of moisture at this level made it harder for plants to thrive. The higher we traveled the smaller the plants. I decided there was a serious message on the ground—the higher you go the harder the going becomes.

The first day we slipped repeatedly on wet roots and mud. This day the footing was better, but we began to encounter some sharp rock. Our running shoes at times proved a bit thin and the feet protested.

This phase of a mountain ascent was, for me, as much a mental adjustment as a physical adjustment. Our pace was steady but not too fast. The terrain was not very exciting and in many hours of slow ascent there is a great deal of time to think. No phones, no interruptions, no meetings, no places to be, just one foot ahead of the other, a rhythmic breathing and a great deal of time to think, dream and remember.

The second day, above 9,000 feet, brought the first real indication of thin air. The climber feels a heavy pull on the lungs and begins more frequent stops for rest. Often one develops a slight headache. It's the brain's way of letting you know it is not getting enough oxygen and does not appreciate it one bit. A wonder drug called aspirin usually works.

I stopped to pop a couple of aspirins and thought of the traditional physician to patient line, "Take two aspirins and call me in the morning." In Africa the line would be, "Take two aspirins and call me anything you like, you're the one who volunteered for all this pleasure."

Our greatest concern in prepping for a climb as high as the summit of Kilimanjaro was altitude sickness. Bill had done some reading of medical articles and had consulted a few physician friends. Our deduction was that in the greatest age of medical discovery in the history of the world not much had been done in the area of altitude sickness, it's physiological causes or treatment. Medicine seemed to be in the 19th Century on the issue.

Dr. John Duckworth, a respected Memphis pathologist, advised through a mutual friend, that a drug called Diamox was the only thing that might help. He stressed the "might." He passed along a friendly warning that Kilimanjaro was a "big league" mountain capable of causing serious harm and possible death from oxygen deprivation.

Bill discovered that the chief of anesthesiology at Presbyterian Hospital in Albuquerque, Dr. Earl Godwin had successfully climbed Kili with his wife Joyce. They made the ascent without the benefit of Diamox. Later, on a three day climb of Mt. Rainier in Washington state, Dr. Godwin had used the drug. He was able to contrast the two experiences and felt that Diamox *was* helpful. He was kind enough to write us a prescription for our attempt on Kilimanjaro.

We began taking Diamox the day before the climb and continued to take it twice a day, each day on the mountain. The side effects were reported to be increased urination and a tingling sensation in the finger tips. Calls of nature, we learned, did not increase in our case, but finger tips did tingle. Our deduction produced a smile: Tinkling same, tingling more.

There was no escaping the persistent, recurring question that bounces around the head of the climber of mountains; would we reach the summit? The question seemed to emerge on the hour.

In 1985 I had my first bout with altitude sickness. The experience haunted me on the Kili climb. Dr. Jim Carman, mentor, dear friend and professor in the graduate school of business at the University of California-Berkeley, called and asked if I would be interested in climbing Mt. Whitney. Jim is one of my heroes in life, so I jumped at the chance to spend some time with him. The mountain was a nice bonus. His wonderful wife and my good friend, Carol had been scheduled to make the trip but had injured a foot, the very definition of de-feet if you are going up a mountain.

I met Jim in Reno, Nevada, we drove south on highway 395 to a trail head near Independence and hiked the John Muir trail for a few days, aided by a mule team. The mule skinner and his girl friend, who doubled as cook, would move ahead on the trail, set up camp, and provide us with scotch, wine and delicious hot food at the end of each day. Jim, being a true scholar with superior intelligence, really knew how to rough it.

In a few days we were on the back side of the 14,495 foot Mt. Whitney, the highest mountain in the 48 states. When we reached 13,000 feet I experienced a severe headache. Aspirin didn't touch it, the headache wouldn't abate. Putting one foot in front of the other was painful. I became very lethargic. My coordination, usually excellent, was definitely impaired. I stumbled and had trouble placing my feet where my eyes and brain indicated they should go. I could take only two or three steps at a time and would literally gasp for breath. Then take two or three steps and gasp again. The slope was not that difficult.

After hours of struggle I finally reached the summit well behind Jim, who seemed just fine. I was terribly depressed and mute at what should have been a glorious moment. The best I could do was slump against a rock and stare with little interest at a magnificent view of the Sierra Mountains. I felt awful, had no appetite and was numb in the wrong places.

Jim, ever watchful and wise, let me rest and then gave the signal to descend. I had many of the classic symptoms of altitude sickness and he knew things would improve on the way down. They did and we finished the trip tired, sore but proud of our accomplishment. All symptoms vanished long before we reached the bottom of the mountain.

Bill had spoken to Jim after our Whitney experience and told Jim we intended to climb Kilimanjaro. Jim expressed studied concern. "He had real trouble at 14,495 on Whitney. What is Patrick going to experience if he tries to to go 18,000 or 19,000?" He was concerned and so was I. Would I be strong enough physically and mentally to overcome the effects of oxygen deprivation in Africa? Would I be tough enough and disciplined enough to push past the symptoms and the pain and continue to the summit? Better question: Would I be disciplined and insightful enough to know when to quit and descend if the symptoms became too pronounced? Many climbers, in their burning quest for the prized and long sought summit, had pushed ahead in spite of multiple symptoms and died in the process.

Bill Jackson is an excellent athlete. His tennis skills had earned him a full ride at the University of Nebraska. He could spot most players an extra serve, give them the doubles line while he took the singles and still win a round of cold ones. I know, for I consistently paid for the beer.

Bill has that quality so important to successful athletes, he is ultimately competitive. This causes him to mask concerns in the spirit of competitive challenge. On the issue of reaching the summit of Kili or failing to reach the summit of Kili, Bill said, "Wouldn't it be a bitch to come this far and work this hard and not make the top? We can't let that happen, big guy. No way."

He took his role as druggist very seriously, dispensing Diamox without fail. We both silently hoped it would help.

The second day wore on, one foot in front of the other, pushing steadily upward with a pause for rest every hour or so. Everyone seemed to be doing well. Bill, Frankie and Bruno tended to lead. Bill rarely followed anyone.

David seemed to work up and down the trail between Dwight and me, spending time at both ends of the team. I took my usual position at the end of the party, just ahead of our chief guide Felix The Quiet, Felix The Pleasant, who purposely anchored our line of march to make sure all in his care remained well and accounted for.

From the skies, I thought, our small single line of climbers must resemble a very small caterpillar, slowly inching ahead, trying to find the top of a very large plant. I decided to interview the caterpillar to see what I could learn.

"Tell me, Mr. Caterpillar, why on earth are you making this slow, tortuous climb?"

"Why, it's what I do, it's my purpose, my reason for being."

"And what do you expect to find when you reach the top?"

"Inquisitive friend, I expect to find the end of something."

"Is that all?"

"Is that all?" said the patient Mr. Caterpillar, "why that is quite enough. But in the end of something I shall also find the beginning of something else."

"And when you reach the top, what then? Will you simply come on down?"

"Come down? Dear, dear, dear man, that's regression and I'll have none of it."

"What then, will you simply stay at the top and look down on life for the rest of your days?"

"No, that's complacency and I've no time for same old, same old. I'm not sure what I will choose to do. But I am sure I will become creative. Maybe I'll have a rest and chew on a new leaf. Perhaps drink a little dew and dream a bit. Never fear, for I will think of something. Something new and different."

The caterpillar paused to rest, lost in new thought. "Yes, I think I will embrace change and . . . perhaps I'll take up flying."

We were now above the clouds. The day was sunny, crisp and clear. Plant life was sparse and unfamiliar.

In the upper meadow, near 11,500 feet, we saw the first of a pre-historic looking plant called giant scenecio. Scenecio cottoni is reportedly found only on Kilimanjaro. The plant, which appears to be a tree without limbs, grows very slowly. At fifteen feet a scenecio could be over 200 years old. We paused to photograph and examine the cottoni. The trunk reminded me of closely knit dried leaves with the texture and tone of a pine cone. At the top of the gently curving trunk there is a green cactus-like plant, sort of a top knot. Sometimes the trunk splits in two near the top and sports two green top knots.

As we continued our slow deliberate pace I did some quick math and determined that the scenecio grows about one foot every thirteen years, less than a inch a year.

Ground cover is sparse at 12,000 feet. I noticed miniature daisies growing in clusters. The daisy is one of my favorite flowers. I love their near perfect symmetry, so clean and neat. The designer must have been Scandinavian, probably a Finn. Finnish design quality is extraordinary. Could God be a Finn, I wondered, with a smile? Nope, couldn't be a Finn, my God has a sense of humor.

I stopped for a closer look. I've photographed daisies in black and white. I once designed a poster for an art festival which consisted of a very large blow up of a single perfect daisy. I've

GIANT SENECIO
(SENECIO COTTONI)

AT 21' A GIANT SENECIO COULD
BE MORE THAN 200 YEARS OLD. THEY
ARE FOUND ON KILIMANJARO AT
12,000 FEET AND GROW VERY SLOWLY.

THE BLACK FUR COVER ON THE
MASAI WARRIOR'S SPEAR
INDICATES PEACE.

·PAT MAGES·

painted daisies in acrylic using a small pallet knife and laying in a petal at a time in thick white. On close examination these African mountain daisies were smaller and more delicate than any I had ever seen, so I dropped to my knees to make a close-up Kodachrome and get in touch with the land.

I soon discovered they were not delicate at all. They were more like leather.

Many months later I learned they are called helichrysum newii—the everlasting flower of Kilimanjaro. Helichrysum are now protected by law and can no longer be picked. I didn't know this at the time but I never pick anything in the delicate environment high on a mountain.

I also learned that in years past every conqueror of the summit of Kili received a garland of these everlasting flowers. The natives carefully wove them with strands of moss and another variety of the daisy-like flower called helicrysum meyeri-johannis. They are said to maintain their color for decades. Tough little flowers. But you've got to be tough to live in this poor volcanic soil at 12,000 feet, much less live and bloom. There is a poem there somewhere, I thought.

The name of the second variety of daisy seemed curious and I checked the table of ascents on Kilimanjaro. Of course, the first climbers to make the summit were Hans Meyer and Kurt Johannes. And there it was—helicrysum meyeri-johannis.

Today, and wisely so, there are no more garlands and the climber brings the flowers home on film.

When we reached Horombo Hut late in the day the porters had a wood fire blazing and the cook was working on a hot meal. The porters had carried fire wood from the rain forest far below our camp.

Dinner was served and it began with a smoky chicken broth, green in color, and sprinkled with bits of herbs. It was tolerable. Then came a platter of boiled potatoes and chicken, which tasted of wood smoke. Also tolerable. The meal was topped off with wood smoked tea. It was amazing how the cook consistently made everything taste like wood smoke. On this trip I would lose twelve pounds. For an American, not a bad thing.

We shared the A-frames at Horombo with a Swiss group, also on their way up the mountain, and with a small group of Americans on their way down. The Swiss were in good spirits and played cards by lantern light to pass the long evening hours. We noted that some of the Americans were not in good spirit. I observed a man in his mid-fifties who sat silently, not moving, head down, obviously dejected, perhaps depressed.

I went over to him and gently inquired about his health. He did not respond. I tried again. No response. I looked around for one of his team members and was told that at base camp the previous night (altitude about 15,500 feet) as the group prepared for the final ascent he had become disoriented, confused and could not form intelligible words. He had babbled excitedly, making no sense at all, just garbled sounds. It was a clear case of altitude sickness, serious oxygen deprivation. They did the right thing and brought him down the mountain as quickly as possible, the only real cure for his condition.

At Horombo Hut he had improved but was depressed and unresponsive. It was clear to me that, while coming down from 15,500 feet to 12,300 had helped, he was still too high and was not getting enough oxygen. Never bashful about offering an opinion, particularly in what I felt was a crisis situation, I urged his team to take him lower at the first possible moment, in the dark if necessary. They huddled, discussed my opinion and decided to wait until morning.

I felt great empathy for the man, who looked fit and appeared to be no stranger to the outdoors or to physical challenge. He had come so far, but could not go on. So close to the summit, but so very far. There would be no summit for him. As painful as it must have been, his team had made the right decision, to bring him down before serious or perhaps irreversible damage was done to his brain. Despondent as he appeared to be, he would live to climb another day. I walked over to him and tried his name. No response. So, I patted his shoulder and whispered in his ear. "Sorry, my friend, but you can come back and try again. The mountain will always be waiting for you."

I joined my group and related the story. The American's misfortune was a substantial jolt of reality. The altitude can shut you down, render you helpless. It had happened to Sir Edmund Hillary, the first to conquer Everest (29,000 feet). Hillary had trouble at 15,400 feet on Kili and descended without reaching the summit. It had happened to Neil Armstrong, the first man on the moon and a very fit astronaut, at about the same altitude. I had a taste of the problem on Mt. Whitney at 14,000 feet.

The agonizing question emerged again. Could we actually do it? Or would some of us suffer a similar fate? I pressed the group to agree that if one of us developed similar problems we would do everything possible to get the climber all the way to the base of the mountain as quickly as possible.

In the dark, David entertained us with tales of his tours of Nepal and India and his trips to the base camp of Mt. Everest at 17,500 feet.

"Don't drink the water" is an expression that took on new meaning for all of us following his tale of an Australian co-driver, who was more than a bit "thick." David cautioned him, as they motored a group of British tourists through India, that he should not drink water directly from a stream no matter how fast it was moving or how fresh it appeared. At one stop David repeated the warning but the "bloke" promptly lowered his head into the stream and drank long and hard. Several days later he began to experience respiratory problems and was hacking and coughing at all hours. David urged him to see a doctor. No deal, said the Aussie, he would hang in there and tough it out. Several days later there was no improvement and he was now bleeding from the nose. He continued to resist treatment. The problem resolved itself one day when a leech crawled out of his nose and dropped onto his breakfast plate. The symptoms quickly vanished, but not the leech. He saved it, carried the dried out thing in his wallet and reportedly gave it to his girlfriend as a memento of his brush with Indian wild life. Mad dogs and Australians, no doubt.

David roared at the telling and a few of us laughed nervously, but most of us around the campfire had at some point on a mountain taken waters directly from a stream and could relate all too well.

The stories continued, but we now added a bit more of Frankie Spite's iodine tablets to our drinking water and, for good measure, added some to the tea as well.

While we were still shaking our heads over David's leech story I steered him to World War II. We spoke of the personal admiration that had existed between President Roosevelt and Winston Churchill. America's entry in the War had turned the tide for the British and played a major role in the defeat of Hitler, Germany and the Axis powers. We agreed there was an unusually strong bond to this day between the United States and Great Britain.

David reminded us that relations between American and British troops had not been so keen during the war. American fighting men, training in England before crossing the English Channel and taking shots at Adolph's boys, took shots at the local ladies, married or not. This, said David, prompted more than a few bitter feelings because the Americans were flush with bucks and were good shooters. He related one of the popular admonishments of the day, spoken with the stiffest of upper lips, "Ah yes, the Yanks, they're over paid, they're over sexed and they're OVER HERE!"

Bruno of Munich, the German climber, was quiet during this discussion of the War. Sensing he was uncomfortable, Dwight of Texas changed the subject and we heard a few Lone Star stories.

When Bruno finally contributed to the conversation he began by pointing out that it was a German who had first conquered Kilimanjaro, his countryman Hans Meyer. He went on to point out that Germans had been the first to conquer most of the summits in the European Alps. We agreed that German climbers were some of the best.

Knowing that I played soccer in a couple of leagues in Memphis, Bruno then reminded me of the power and skill of German "futball" teams. He pointed out that the Bundislega, the famous German professional soccer league, was one of the finest and most competitive in the world. He made a point that the Germans had won the World Cup of soccer more than once and America had rarely even qualified for Cup competition. He threw in a mention of the Olympics and the generally superior quality of German track and field athletes. A few of us agreed, without much enthusiasm, that German football was some of the best.

It became quiet around the old campfire.

Bruno was on a roll. He then began talking about classical music, his favorite, and the tremendous contributions made by German composers. He went on and on about the wonder of Wagner's four opera group "The Ring Of The Nibelung" and it's powerful dramatic tones. David was the lone voice agreeing that Wagner was certainly a master. I had my money on Edward Kennedy "Duke" Ellington, but didn't go there.

It was extremely quiet around the campfire.

Before young Bruno Schmidt could select another superior German contribution to the world, and extol the virtues of Germany once again, a voice, which sounded very much like mine said, "But Bruno, in the 20th Century Germany is 0 and 2 in wars."

This stunned the group and there was an embarrassed silence before suppressed chuckles and much head shaking began to infect the assembled. No one looked at Bruno. I had expected some anger, but Bruno simply looked confused. When I had spoken the phrase it came out "oh and two" not "zero and two" or "nil and two," which he might have understood.

"Vas is dis oh and two?" said Bruno.

With a definite smile in his voice Bill jumped in. "It means no victories and two defeats."

Bill then emitted his high pitched shriek followed by his roaring laugh. His eyes were dancing. No one loves a good put down better than Bill. His Jack Nicholson smile was at 50 megawatts. He reached over and gave me a high five and the conversation was over.

On the war score we all turned in. War crimes and mountaineering do not mix well. National pride is quite another matter. But hubris is unacceptable. Particularly when you start two wars and lose two wars.

As I made my way to an A-frame shelter I walked over to the American climber who was still sitting in the same place, head down, depressed and defeated. I patted him on the shoulder again and told him he would be much better tomorrow.

He did not respond. I lay awake wondering if brain damage had already been done. I resolved that in a similar situation I would have taken him all the way down the mountain, regardless of the dark or the weather, to the rich oxygen saturated air of the rain forest.

Sleeping in the mountains is a quest for dry and warm. Bless the Norwegian mountaineers who had built the huts. They were simple and effective. While the wood floor was hard, a Thermarest inflatable mattress, a popular item which provides only a half inch of cushion, was just enough to provide some small comfort. It's real value is insulation. It puts the mountaineer above cold, damp ground and preserves body heat.

I noted, while packing up at Mandara Hut in the morning, the wood under my Thermarest was actually warm. Body heat had penetrated the mattress and warmed the floor boards. Would it be enough to dry wet clothing? Interesting thought. I decided to experiment and placed a damp t-shirt and shorts under the pad. Perhaps they would be dry in the morning. I then crawled into my Blue Kazoo sleeping bag and noted once more that it is impossible to say "Blue Kazoo" without smiling.

I'm a late person and always have trouble with the early bed time hours on a mountain. I rolled from side to side, still wide awake. My nose was inches away from the wall of the A-frame and I could detect the faint smell of cedar.

How many climbers had rested in my spot, thinking about the top of the mountain and the test of will it requires to get there? How many, I wondered, had remained awake in this humble but magnificent dwelling and thought about home, a warm, clean, familiar bed, dry clothes, food that didn't taste of wood smoke, and a reassuring hug. How many climbers had questioned the wisdom of a trip across the African plain and a punishing climb of Kili? I concluded that if you didn't question your judgment you certainly were not in normal range—flat brain waves for sure.

Bruno was sleeping peacefully, just inches away. Dwight was snoring lightly. I was wide awake, brain waves dancing.

One hundred years ago, a young Hans Meyer had probably tossed and turned in Liepzig, Germany on the eve of another journey to Africa and his third attempt at Kilimanjaro. He would sail and walk from Europe to East Africa to attempt the summit—a more difficult journey than ours by many leagues. No Boeing 747 at 550 knots per hour from London to Nairobi, no four wheel drive trucks, no Thermarest, no Diamox, no A-frame shelters.

Go to sleep, Patrick, go to sleep. This is the Presidential Suite at the Marriott compared to what Mr. Meyer experienced. I was actually sleeping higher on Kili than he climbed on his first ascent in 1887.

I woke up mid-way through the night with a very strong need to urinate. I was warm and it would be damn cold outside the bag and even colder outside the shelter. Fight it. Do not get up. Wait till morning, said the brain. But the rest of the body protested. Nature wins again. She usually does.

I found the tab of the zipper on my sleeping bag and began to open it very slowly to minimize the noise. In the supreme quiet of the high mountain it sounded like a train. Once out of the bag I found my shoes and gently, quietly opened the door. Just then I heard Bruno's zipper and thought, "Hell's bells, I woke him up after all." It turned out that Bruno was on the same mission. Just as Bruno pulled on his shoes, we heard Dwight's zipper . . . . three for three. In hushed voices we emerged from the A-frame and found the designated spot for emission. Looking up we were astounded by the star filled night, more stars than any of us had ever seen. We marveled at the dark beauty and pissed in unison.

Back in the shelter, shoes hit the floor, clunk, clunk, clunk and bags were closed to a zip, zip, zip. What teamwork.

A voice in the dark from the other side of the shelter, which sounded very much like a guy from Albuquerque, said, "Hey, what the hell is this guys, a new team sport?"

We all enjoyed a laugh. Nothing I know creates bonding better than a good laugh, particularly when laughing at yourself.

Day three of the ascent of Kilimanjaro
Saturday, June 6th

To The Kibo Base Camp—12,300 to 15,400 Feet

It had only been a few minutes between the gentle Felix wake-up knock and the uncomfortable process of leaving a warm sleeping bag and fighting night's inflicted stiffness of back and limbs. I literally crawled out the door and onto the steps of the hut to see what Kili was giving us. The mountain was giving us beauty this day. Unsurpassed, unrestrained, unqualified beauty. I sat there wondering how I could be so fortunate.

Far, far below my lofty perch the world resembled slowly rolling dark gray cotton batten. It seemed as if the artist wanted a dull soft backdrop for the bold, bright strokes to come. Above the dull gray of slowly boiling cloudy downe, was the crystalline shimmer and sparkle of dew over patches of green and straw colored ground cover, set against the clearest, cleanest, deepest blue sky eyes have ever seen.

The upper mountain was glazed in white-gold strokes of early morning sun. The sun signaled spirits-up and soaring.

The startling contrast was framed in perfect silence. One held one's breath so as not to intrude and break the spell.

How

clear, how

very clear the

mountain is today.

It is hard to imagine

the mountain being any other

way. How still, how very still,

all senses are awake. But the only

sound you hear is the very sound you make.

My arms embraced my chest, hands buried against the chill. I listened carefully to my shallow breathing and reveled in the thrill . . . . of sitting on the shoulders of a giant and matching my will against the mountain.

David had been up and out early and had ordered the ritual hot tea, which the porters brought very swiftly. They also brought their version of hot cereal. I tried it once again, this time with lots of sugar.

Everyone was feeling good. Bruno, Dwight and I took some good natured kidding about our team effort during the night. There is nothing at all private about living together on a mountain. One must become pretty blasé about body functions and basic needs.

We left Horombo Hut about 8:30 AM. We faced a full days trek of 9.3 miles, all of it up and through high alpine desert, across ancient lava fields to the edge of a frozen desert and the base camp called Kibo Hut. It was a pivotal day. Bill and I had never been higher on a mountain than 14,495 feet. We would pass our personal best during this trek, with an altitude gain of 3,100 feet.

Just north of Horombo Hut we crossed a small stream. A simple wooden marker informed us that this was the last water. From here on up everyone would carry water.

The porters passed us on the trail. Well acclimated, they were taking two steps to our one. Bless them for they were carrying firewood and enough water for cooking and tea. They would build a fire at 15,400 feet, our base camp for the final ascent. While we labored up the steepest part of the mountain to the summit, they would stay at base camp and keep the home fire burning.

One of the porters was carrying a large bouquet of leafy plants. He carried them much the way one would take flowers to a best girl. Is it a ritual, I wondered? Is he superstitious? Is it a gift for the Gods of the Kilimanjaro crater?

It turned out to be nothing so exotic or mystical. He was carrying herbs for soup and tea, picked many miles below and carried by hand to dry as he hiked up the mountain. An herb bearer! Take that, Sam Clemens. So much for your Latinist and bar tenders, our expedition had an herb bearer. How perfectly classy.

I have more than a passing interest in herbs, the result of a life-long interest in cooking. I've been growing and drying herbs for many years. Just outside my door I have pots of chive, basil, oregano, rosemary and thyme. I can look up from the pages of a Julia Child recipe and in a few steps be snipping the required fresh herbs. If a dish doesn't look finished or a presentation looks dull I can remedy the situation in seconds with sprigs of fresh herbs.

As we continued through featureless high desert I gave further thought to our native cook. If only I could teach him a culinary trick or two.

I designed a Gary Larsen cartoon: the white tourist chef in a pith helmet is instructing the native cooks of Kili. The tourist chef is standing inside a five-foot deep cooking pot, with water up to his chest. A large wood fire is roaring under the pot. He is holding a small ladle and has just tasted the broth. "More herbs, gentlemen, more herbs, BUT spare the salt, it's bad for my heart."

For the first time during our long slow trek we passed porters who were on their way down. They were smiling.

We exchanged the customary Swahili greeting of East Africa.

"Jambo!"

"Jambo!" I replied.

"Habari," returned the native.

"Mizuri," I replied.

The free translation is:

"Hello."

"Hello."

"How are you?"

"Fine, thank you."

The pattern is always the same and it nearly becomes a chant.

Jambo	(jam-bow)
Habari	(ha-bar-ee)
Mizuri	(Miss-ouri)

Jambo

Habari

Mizuri

Jambo

Habari

Mizuri

The greeting had become automatic. If we saw a black face on the trail we did the jambo, habari, mizuri exchange. When a white face appeared we reverted to English, "Hello, how are you this morning?"

A short distance out of Horombo we passed more native porters and began to exchange the jambo greeting. Suddenly a white face appeared. I said "Good morning." I received a "Good day to you" in a clipped British accent.

There is something special about the people you meet on mountains, I thought, as the volcanic sand crunched under foot. At this stage of my life I had been walking up mountains, scrambling up mountains and even crawling up mountains for about ten years. I had been on mountains in every weather condition, in five states, three countries and three continents. I would survive to eventually visit mountains on five of the seven continents. The people I've met on mountains have consistently been very nice people.

Other mountaineers are often few and far between on remote mountains. When you do encounter someone up high all are willing to talk, advise, inquire or offer helpful tips and warnings without any prompting. Those on the way down are invariably willing to share the elation of a successful ascent and cheer you on. There are offers to share food or drink and other necessary provisions. There is a sincere exchange of concern for one another's health and safety and there is an unmistakable camaraderie.

Over several beers one night in Aspen, Colorado I was discussing this phenomena with several far more experienced mountaineers. "I've never met a jerk on a mountain," I said.

"Hey," came the response, "there are no assholes in the mountains."

We raised our pints and drank to that pithy statement of fact.

Language differences? Gender? Nationality? Political orientation? Economic background? Education? Social status? None of it matters in the mountains. The mountains are an incredible equalizer. They do not discriminate. They punish everyone. And they reward everyone willing to take the punishment along with the beauty.

Why Climb A Mountain?

Why climb a mountain? I've heard this question dozens of times. I've learned it is as much a statement as it is a question. The friend or acquaintance is expressing an opinion. It isn't disapproval; it is simply concern for human life based on their perception that climbing a mountain is a needlessly dangerous act with little or no redeeming social value.

It is interesting to note that the daily act of getting behind the wheel of an automobile and taking to city streets, where one is at the mercy of hundreds of on-coming drivers, with varied attention spans, judgment and driving skills, is far more dangerous than climbing a mountain.

But the question remains, why do we climb? Many mountaineers prefer to duck the question on the premise that climbing mountains is not something to talk about; it is something to experience, to do. George Leigh Mallory, a leading English climber of his day, made several attempts to become the first to reach the summit of Mt. Everest. He failed on his first two attempts in the early 1920's. When pressed by reporters to explain why he would attempt something as dangerous as an ascent of the world's highest mountain, he grew tired of the question and flippantly replied, "Because it's there!"

Later he provided a more thoughtful answer, which is rarely quoted: "To struggle and to understand."

There are many reasons for climbing mountains. While they are interwoven and suggest a certain spirit within the soul, they are reasons worth describing as individual thoughts.

Climbing a mountain is first a test of physical and mental endurance. Ascending a mountain can be a struggle of great proportion. The ascent teaches me my limits and I find I am often more capable of greater mind and body endurance than I ever dreamed. I struggle and develop a better understanding of who I am.

Climbing a mountain can certainly put one's life at risk. Once the risk has been taken, with reason and good judgment, and the climb has been completed successfully, growth and increased self-confidence are the benefits. I discover that I have courage I didn't fully recognize or appreciate. The risk, successfully taken in the climb of a high mountain, also increases my appreciation for life in all its forms, in all its moments. What, you say, is a successful climb, a successful risk? It is the climb you come back from.

George Mallory made a final attempt at Mt.Everest in 1924. He and his climbing partner, Andrew Irvine disappeared less than a thousand feet from the summit. For over seventy years their fate was unknown until a team of climbers found Mallory's well-preserved body in a snowfield far below the summit, where it had come to rest after a long and lethal fall. Mallory and Irvine had the courage and they took the risk, but mountains can be very unforgiving. A mistake, in this case resulting in a fall, cost them their lives.

Climbing a mountain satisfies insatiable curiosity. If you have it, you must go up. In fact, history is replete with man's pursuit of the unknown. It is clear to me that one of the enduring principles in life is that everything . . . . everything must be tried, everything must be explored, every risk must be taken, every challenge met. This principle has permitted mankind to grow and improve and improve and grow, ever more. The driving question is, what will we find at the summit, what will the summit show us, what will reaching the summit teach us?

There are many cartoons suggesting that the summit of every mountain is home to a guru in white robes sitting in the lotus position and pontificating. In one of my favorite cartoons, drawn by Johnny Hart the creator of B.C., the climber struggles to the summit on his hands and knees and finds the guru.

"What question do you have for me?" says the guru.

Gasping, the climber asks, "What is the meaning of life?"

Responds the guru, "Why it's just one damned thing after the other, I thought everyone knew that!"

Climbing a mountain is a search for great natural beauty, beauty that is raw and powerful. Mountains create their own weather and it is not uncommon to experience all types of weather in a single climb. Add changing weather to the incredible vistas of a high mountain and you experience awe-inspiring beauty. I have, on many occasions, felt the beauty of a mountain well in my eyes and produce warm tears.

John Muir, our first heralded environmentalist, spoke of the powerful beauty: "The minister will not preach a perfectly flat and sedimentary sermon after climbing a snowy peak."

Climbing a mountain provides an indelible sense of achievement. Mankind must have a sense of purpose or life may not seem worth living. Achievement gives us the sense that our life has value. Achievement is fuel for the mind, the heart and the soul.

I have spent much of my life in organizations, mostly trying to make life better for managers, employees and customers. I've often spent weeks and months laboring over a leadership or management problem, the design of a better product or service, or the resolution of conflict between employees and customers. Some days these organizational challenges and a disheartening lack of progress make me wonder if I've achieved anything at all.

Ahh, but once you have labored long and hard to reach the summit of a high mountain and gone where comparatively few people will ever go; no one can take that achievement from you. It can't be tabled, referred to a committee, sent to three layers of higher authority for approval or anesthetized by a board of directors. The achievement is yours. You got there using your skill and your will and your good judgment. No one can dilute or destroy the sense of accomplishment. The moment of achievement, always captured on film at the summit, is yours forever.

Finally, climbing a high mountain is inspiring. The struggle, the beauty, the sense of achievement and the increased self confidence inspires us to do more.

The late Charles Kuralt, host of the CBS presentation "Sunday Morning," understood the powerful affect of the mountains. "Mountains have a hold on us," said Kuralt, in his deep baritone. "They inspire awe. Where did Moses talk to God? Why, on a mountain."

Climbing a mountain is about many things: it is a test of physical and mental endurance, putting life at risk and finding one's level of courage, satisfying curiosity and the need to explore, a search for natural beauty, and understanding who you are and what you are made of.

Mallory may have said it best, after all, "To struggle and to understand."

I always feel a special duty to bring back the stories and the photographs and share them with family, friends, and anyone with an interest in learning about an adventure they will never pursue, or a place they will never go. In a small way I can bring an unusual part of the world to people, share the joy of reaching the summit and enrich some lives with my experience.

We reached 13,500 feet and the sparse vegetation began to disappear. We entered a high desert of volcanic sand and, while the grass was all but gone, I could still find very small clumps of helicrysum and wondered, once again, how they managed to survive.

The scene ahead was bleak. Sand, sand and more sand, punctuated by a few large black rocks scattered here and there.

The group maintained a comfortable, steady pace in spite of the altitude gain. I noted that I had begun taking deliberate deep breaths every five minutes or so. We moved on in silence working our way up the gradual shoulder of Kili, hoping to acclimate, hoping the heart, lungs, brain and muscles would adjust. We were now two and one half miles above sea level.

We pushed up the slope. Crunch, crunch, crunch. Plenty of time to think while putting one foot in front of the other. Time for a running stream of thought. Time for important self-motivation.

As I plodded along my thoughts returned to the survival of the leather-like daisies. They represented a serious paradigm shift. Flowers are delicate and fragile, something I had learned as a child. Later in life I learned that flowers in a high mountain meadow on the edge of a frozen desert are very tough little flowers.

My thoughts shifted to another flower lesson, this one taught by a child high in the Colorado Rockies. I was visiting an ecologist, teacher, country philosopher and mountain man named Stewart Maize. He lived at a compound called Toklat, high above Aspen. This day he was entertaining a group of elementary school children. He was introducing them to the plants, flowers and wild life in the meadows near his home in an effort to establish respect for the fragile environment of the high mountains.

One of the children tugged on his arm and asked Stewart if flowers could talk?

"Why no," said the patient Mr. Maize, "flowers can't actually talk, but they do speak to us in a sense with their beauty, their scent and color."

What a nice answer, I thought. He is remarkable.

"Can too talk," said another little voice.

The mountain man smiled his fatherly smile. "Can they now? Well, that is good news young man. Tell us, what do flowers say?"

"When you step on 'em they say 'crunch.'"

I looked at Stewart. He looked at me. I was speechless, he was not.

"Why, indeed they do, indeed they do say 'crunch.' But we don't want them to say 'crunch' do we children?" said the consummate teacher.

The kids responded with a chorus of "noooooooo."

Stewart turned away from the kids and looked up the mountains for a moment. When he turned back to face the children I saw the mist in his eyes . . . and the joy. It was one of those moments in life you do not forget, a moment you cherish.

I pulled out my ever present note pad and recorded the dialogue. I would not forget this lesson. What a blessing, I thought, if one could hang on to the childlike wonder, the uninhibited, unencumbered and totally honest view of kids. Oh that we could inject a little of that child-like quality into adults. Would the planet be a better place? Only infinitely.

Step, step, step up the sandy desert slope, with a pause now and then to draw some breath and scan the bleak landscape which began to remind me of scenes from a lunar landing. You can have any color today as long as it is brown. Brown in several subtle tones, but brown as far as the eye can see. "Hey, Bill," I shouted, "this must be Albuquerque, endless shades of brown." Bill told me to do something physically impossible.

The plains far below were obstructed by clouds. We were left with no view to speak of, just the bleak landscape with large black rocks scattered here and there. As I was about to pronounce the vista dull, duller, dullest, it occurred to me that the rocks were randomly scattered across the high desert sand and they sat alone with no smaller rocks around them. Curious.

I began examining the black rocks. They were about five feet in diameter and perhaps six or seven feet in height. The longer I observed them the more I concluded that they looked out of place, like crude marbles on a tan carpet. They didn't seem to belong to anything. There was no rock strata pushing up beneath them. They were not connected to a foundation of rock formations. They rested individually on the surface of the desert. It was as if a giant hand had picked them up somewhere and placed each one on the sand. Very curious, indeed. I photographed the scene and promised to give it more thought.

Many months later I was drawn to a passage in a description of Mt. Kilimanjaro by a scientist who explained that the rocks I somehow thought were curious and didn't belong where they very permanently rested are actually lava bombs, blown into the sky in a Kili eruption. They have been decorating the high shoulders of the mountain for centuries.

Imagine globs of molten lava blown into the cold sky, cooling on the fly, tumbling, being shaped by the wind into round forms and landing on the sand in a natural random pattern to harden and rest forever. It was the hail storm from hell.

From memories of a childhood visit to a colonial village in Pennsylvania, I suddenly recalled seeing a shot tower. Shot, for the long smooth bore rifles of the colonial era, was made by taking molten metal to the top of a shot tower several stories high and allowing drops of metal to fall through the air, shaping into spheres in flight and splashing into a pool of cold water at ground level. Once hardened, the metal balls were carried in deerskin pouches until they were tamped down the barrel of a black powder muzzle loader and readied for beast or foe.

The "shot" on Kili was rather large stuff.

Step, step, step, past the lava rocks, constantly moving upward, constantly working the mind, pushing the climber ahead.

On a climb of Mt. Olympus in Washington State I was overtaken by a storm that moved up the mountain behind me. There was no shelter, no escape. The storm brought lightening and hail, large hail. I was well equipped. In addition to a metal framed back pack I was toting an ice axe, crampons, carabineers and many cans of fuel for melting snow and cooking. In essence, I was a well-crafted lightening rod.

There was nowhere to go. All I could do was strip off anything with metal, move away from it, crouch, tuck my head and hope, wish, or pray the lightening would strike elsewhere, preferably an "elsewhere" some distance away. Maybe in another country.

The lightening moved past but I was pelted for many minutes by large hail. I'm certain the size of anything increases greatly when you are being hit by it, however this was the largest hail I had ever seen. As I slowly worked my way through the high desert of Kili I now thought the Mt. Olympus hail was child's play. Just imagine being caught under a storm of lava bombs the size of a small car. The absurdity of this comparison made me wonder again about the effect of oxygen deprivation on one's sense of perspective.

I continued moving ahead, one foot in front of the other, mostly in silence. The challenge, at this stage on a mountain, is to keep moving, maintain a steady pace and overcome the boredom that can develop. I reminded myself that this stage is the necessary prelude to the real climb. It is a question of slowing working up to base camp, allowing the body to acclimate, and preparing for the final challenge—the severe pitch of the final 3,500 feet to the summit. Hard to imagine boredom at 13,500 feet on one of the world's great mountains? Trust me, it happens when your head is down for hours and you are watching the ground and taking slow, deliberate steps. Thankfully, we have thought, imagination, recall and good memories to fuel the soul and fire the engine.

Our team was strung out with sometimes 100 yards between climbers. Frankie, Bill and Bruno, as usual, were in the lead. I am the perpetual straggler, at the end of the line, but just ahead of the ever watchful Felix The Guide. It was very quiet. The crunch of shoe against volcanic sand was the only sound. The only sound you hear is the sound you make.

David Shrock slowed his pace and joined me. We walked together for about an hour. I had grown very fond of David. He has an irrepressible good nature and shows genuine concern for your interests and ideas. He listens well, which is the ultimate compliment.

David has the Irish fair skin and a shock, as opposed to a Shrock, of curly black hair. His dark eyes are constantly smiling. His mind is a lot like Data Base Bill—quick, full and capable of amazing recall. Unlike Bill, David is the ultimate diplomat. Both Bill and David have a quality I admire greatly, they can converse on an incredibly wide range of subjects. It is an exciting quality, one I constantly seek and rarely find.

David's interests are unlimited. He is an ideal companion for a long, slow mountain ascent. While our meeting in East Africa was pure luck, he is the person you would choose to be with on a climb this high.

We decided on a rest stop near one of the lava bombs. Someone had turned the rock into a trail marker. On the far side of the rock it read "14,500." Since the message was in feet, not meters, we deducted it must be an American notation.

I was excited. "Mr. Schrock, we are at fourteen five and that tops my personal best."

"Well done, mate, so this is your highest, is it?" David offered his hand and I shook it and shouted the news to Bill. This was also his personal best. We had both done Mt. Whitney in California, the highest in the 48 states at 14,495. We had a new personal best by all of five whole feet.

I explained to David that I had gotten into trouble and experienced great altitude sickness on Whitney.

"And you've been worried about how your tolerance of high altitude on Kili. Of course. But you seem remarkable calm and fit. How do you feel now?"

"I feel great. Seriously. No trouble. I feel good. What do you think, David? Is it the slow pace, the gradual acclimatization, the Diamox, better conditioning or just plain luck?"

"All of the above, mate, all of the above." He laughed.

I remembered Bill's conversation with our friend Jim Carman. When Bill explained our intent to do Kili, Jim expressed great concern. "Pat had real trouble on Whitney at 14,000 feet. How is he going to handle 19,000?" As usual, Dr. Carman asks superior questions.

The answer was clear. At 14,500, Pat was doing just fine.

As we pushed along, David reminded us of our ascent tactic by speaking the Swahili warning, "Pole, pole, mates."

Pole (pronounced pole-e, with a long e) means "slowly." Pole, pole (usually said twice), slowly, slowly is wisdom. Allow the body to adjust, let the machinery work and by all means resist the temptation to charge ahead or rush the ascent.

I've seen it happen to first time climbers. They see the summit and catch what is called "peak bagging fever." They want to notch the summit and push or race ahead. I've been passed by many climbers over the years, only to meet them later propped against a rock, exhausted and frustrated . . . or on the way down.

Robert Lange, in his book *Kilimanjaro*, warns of the consequences of storming a mountain this big.

> "By now, with the sighting of the beckoning ice cap [the summit of Kilimanjaro], the desire to press on becomes overwhelming. 'Pole, pole' slowly, slowly the guides constantly have to warn, trying to encourage the climbers to adopt a disciplined, comfortable pace. They have an understandable interest in bringing their charges to the summit and really do know better. Anyone not listening to their advice, treating the ascent as some sort of race to the top, runs the risk of not reaching the ultimate goal."

We will not rush the summit. We will creep up on the monster and take it quietly. And then the caterpillar appears . . . and winks at me.

We stop for a light lunch. Bill and Bruno hate the small bruised Tanzanian oranges we receive at breakfast. As a result, I inherit a good supply. The oranges do not look much like American oranges. They have thicker skin and are not as juicy. Their skin is a faded orange with green spots. But they taste like an orange, they have natural sugar, and are safer than drinking the water.

Bill observes that it has become noticeably colder and attributes this to the fact that we are not moving. We all slip on an extra layer—wind shells or sweaters. We began the ascent almost three days ago in what was a hot, humid summer day in the jungle. It now felt like a late fall day.

We faced up hill and began to move ahead once again. It would take several more hours to reach Kibo hut, our base camp for the real test—an extremely steep pitch and 3,500 feet to the summit.

Mawensi

The only visual relief from volcanic sand and lava rocks was a black jagged formation called Mawensi. It appeared to be a mountain on a mountain, for it rises out of the shoulder of Kilimanjaro and reaches 16,900 feet. Geologists have concluded that Mawensi is not a volcano but rather a lava plug in what was a main vent in the great Kilimanjaro volcano. Lava, under incredible pressure, broke through the crust of the mountain, oozed out of a vent and pushed up several thousand feet before it cooled off and created Mawensi.

According to Felix, Mawensi is a technical climb. It's sides are sheer and the basalt rock is very brittle. Climbers going up Mawensi must secure ropes to the wall and pull themselves up using rock climbing techniques.

Rock falls are frequent on most mountains but must be very frequent on Mawensi. There are great skree piles at the base of this baby brother mountain. Scree is small pieces of rock which break off the mass of a mountain as freezing and thawing occurs. It reminds me of large gravel and is very unstable unless frozen. If it is not frozen and slides it can easily snap an ankle.

Felix pointed to the jagged teeth of the summit. "Many have been killed there. Mawensi bad rock. Climbers fall."

For hundreds of years the Wachagga natives called this peak Kimawensi—the jagged or cracked one. The mountain has eroded over the centuries and the name has eroded as well. It is now spoken of simply as Mawensi.

Lange, in his book *Kilimanjaro,* refers to Mawensi as a volcano. Whether it is a vent that oozed lava from the Kili volcano or a separate volcano, the thought that the inner earth can heat rock to a molten state and then push it through the crust of the earth to run on the land like red hot cement, is a very frightening image.

I watched Mawensi as we climbed in the late afternoon light. It was quiet, no gas or vapors visible. I felt as if we were tip toeing around a sleeping monster.

How Mountains Were Born

Bruno Gutman, an early German explorer of Kilimanjaro, studied the natives that inhabit the jungles and slopes of the mountain. He heard and translated many native tales and fables, including one about the birth of mountains.

> *"How the mountain came into being. Ages*
> *ago the earth was everywhere flat and*
> *uniform. Then it rose in order to speak*
> *to the sky. As it departed again it did not*
> *return home in all places at once. The parts*
> *which got tired on the way home failed to*
> *complete the descent and remained where*
> *they were. These became the earth's*
> *mountains and hills."*

Fables are much more fun than scientific explanations. Got tired on the way down, did they? I buy it. I can relate to tired and refusing to come down.

Kibo Hut

We had been moving across bleak desert all day, one foot in front of the other, up, up and up. Pole, pole. It was now cold and what little sun there was cast long shadows. I struggled up a sharp slope moved around a lava outcropping and arrived, with no visible warning, at Kibo Hut, our base camp at 15,400 feet, and our final resting place before the real adventure. The thrill of reaching base camp was short lived. It had now become very cold indeed. The constant movement through the day had pumped heat through our bodies. Now it would be a struggle to keep warm. Kibo Hut would be our home for about eight hours . . . and then we would leave for the summit.

There are rituals in every sport which signal a commitment to a contest. I reached into my pack and brought out my sturdy Pivetta mountain boots. We had saved our boots for the final ascent when we would need the ankle support and the heavy lug soles. My boots were well seasoned, the leather dark and pliable. Dirt from countless mountains and trails on three continents was permanently sealed in from numerous applications of Snow-seal, a waxy water-proofing product. I donned heavy ragg wool socks and began to lace up my boots. This climber was definitely going up. I would now be adding the soil of Africa to the leather of my mountain boots—the dirt of Kilimanjaro. Somehow this line doesn't seem as dramatic as Hemingway's line, "the snows of Kilimanjaro." It is well that he wrote his line first.

Light was fading fast as we pulled on dry clothes, wool hats and gloves and hooded parkas smelling of moth balls and the Kibo Hotel supply room. Preservation of body heat was now a real issue.

I wanted one last picture before nightfall. I asked Bill to take a position below the Kibo Hut ridge permitting me to photograph him against the broken black teeth of Mawensi. He gamefully trudged down the slope, an effort at this altitude, took up a William The Conqueror pose and pushed his parka hood back. In my Nikon viewfinder I could see Bill in the foreground and the impressive profile of Mawensi poking through very dense clouds which were now ringing the mountain about 1000 feet below us at 14,500 feet. We were very high, in cold, thin air with weather moving up the mountain. Bill was smiling his Cheshire Cat smile, the smile that says, "I know something you don't know."

I advanced the film slowly, a good idea when operating a camera in very cold conditions, and instinctively turned to look up the mountain to see what Bill was seeing. No wonder Jackson was smiling. He was looking above my head at a perfectly clear, sun drenched view of the snow capped Kilimanjaro summit. Mist and clouds had cleared long enough to give us one precious and fleeting glimpse of the white roof of Africa.

I stared with a sense of awe and wonder. My heart literally began pounding in the excitement of seeing the top of Kili for the first time. It did not look that far away. We were close, ever so close. I could make out detail. Ice and snow gripped the edges of the summit, the beginning of the glaciers that move down into the volcano crater. Between masses of snow and ice there were patches of dark brown rock which could provide our path to the summit.

The gods of Kili were teasing us. Or was it motivation? Weather moved aside just for a few minutes and provided a flash of mountain peak. Then night slowly moved in and wrapped its arms tightly around the top of the legendary Kilimanjaro . . . and dared us to come find it.

Base Camp

Spirits were high in spite of the intense cold. It was now early evening. We would not see the sun for another twelve hours. In that time we would do our best to eat, hydrate and get some sleep before setting out for the summit. It had taken us three long days to reach base camp. In a few more hours we would find out if our bodies and minds had acclimated to the altitude.

We drank hot tea, which rather quickly turned into iced tea, and ate what we could.

I have always found it difficult to eat at high altitude. Conventional wisdom would lead one to believe that the sustained effort of moving up a mountain would make a climber very hungry. Not so in my case. I have to force myself to pack calories in at high altitude.

We huddled together in the dark and the talk soon turned to altitude. Everyone had a story or a concern. Bruno indicated he was feeling good. Kibo Hut was his personal high. Frankie and David had been to base camp on Mt. Everest, 17,500 feet in Nepal. They were feeling fine at 15,400 feet on Kili. Dwight, Bill and I had never been higher than 14,400 and felt surprisingly good.

But the all-consuming question remained; could we put six climbers on the top of the mountain and bring them down safely?

"Everyone is feeling good, 'eh mates? Let's not forget to take it slow and easy, pole, pole. Let's not rush it and we'll have a good show of it."

David's words were reassuring and his logic was totally acceptable to all. We agreed that we would have to set the pace and not allow the guides, however well intentioned, to push us too hard or we might not make it. The guides, we reminded one another, had been doing this climb for years. With the possible exception of Bill, who lives in Albuquerque, New Mexico at 4,000 feet, the guides had also spent their lives at an altitude much higher than the rest of us. They had the home field advantage.

The stone shelter we attempted to sleep in was a meat locker. It was pitch black and dead cold. Sleep was an illusive concept.

I recalled the comments made in Hilary Brandt's book, *Backpacker's Africa*. It was a terse description of a night at Kibo Hut. "Few people actually sleep," she wrote. "The night is bitter cold and the lack of oxygen makes sleep difficult even if you're not suffering from the headache and nausea of altitude sickness."

Crawling into my sleeping bag I mumbled something about truth in advertising. I was more than fully clothed and pulled my wool watch cap over my ears and eyes and zipped the bag all the way to the top, leaving a little room for my nose to poke out and pull in what little oxygen there was.

Bill, Dwight and Bruno did pretty much the same. We were all trying to capture and retain as much body heat as possible. The fight to stay warm was on.

David and Frankie, on the other hand, were busy pulling off their outer layers of clothing and placing them under their sleeping bags. Normally this results in wrinkled but warm clothing in the morning. I could not imagine why they were removing clothing.

In a stroke of genuine inspiration, David moved his sleeping bag next to Frankie's and carefully arranged them into one large sleeping bag so they could sleep together. What genius. They proceeded to twist and turn and wiggle their way into the bags. After much commotion full of fumbling and zipping they finally both exhaled and signaled to one and all that the nest was done. All in the meat locker were silent.

I could not help but smile, in spite of the intense cold. Was it lust? Or was it survival? Surely lust is quick to freeze. But, of course, the promise of a thaw is strong. I pictured the two of them in a spoon-like position, arms and legs wrapped together. And could not resist a comment.

"Not fair, not fair at all David Shrock. You picked the best looking lady in the expedition." Laughter.

Evidently the Schrock-Spite body language also translated into German. The next voice was Bruno, a surprise indeed. You could hear the smile in his otherwise serious voice. "It's good, good thing David. I . . . . um . . . not so lucky." Laughter.

The irrepressible Jackson was next. "Let's not see any motion over there, mate buddy. No motion or I throw the flag . . . fifteen yards, illegal motion." Jackson's laughter was louder than the rest.

Dwight weighed in. "All right, David's a happy camper, aren't you, David? He's a veeeeerrrrrrrry happy camper." Laughter.

Silence.

"There, there, it's all right mates, this is PURELY for survival now . . . . isn't it?"

Even in our cold dark-as-ink-well shelter you could see David's smile.

Earlier, in a marathon joke session, David had described Australian and New Zealand sexual foreplay. In a heavy, working class accent designed to needle Frankie, David had given her an exaggerated elbow in the side and said, "Oy, you awake?"

Even Masters and Johnson would have seen the humor.

Silence in the meat locker. It was so cold there was no chance of sleep. Sleep was simply out of the question, a wish. I found I had to squint to keep my eyes closed. It was an effort to pretend sleep.

Silence. Not a motion. Not a breath. Silence for many moments. And then some gentle rustling from the Shrock-Spite nest.

"Oy, you awake?"

The tension of lying in the cold and struggling to make time pass was broken and the darkness became bright with laughter. David! Bless David.

Laughter died at the soft knock on the door of the shelter. Felix was there but we couldn't see him. We looked in the direction of his voice.

"Ah, I will come at midnight to wake you. We have hot tea and then we go."

He paused to let the words register.

"Are you well? All well?"

We assured him that we were "well" and definitely missing central heating. It then dawned on me that Felix lived in a wooden hut and didn't have a clue about central heating.

"All good. Good. You rest and we will have good climb."

As silently and softly as he had come, he was gone.

My feet were like ice. My hands, buried inside a sleeping bag and inside my clothing were numb with cold. The tip of my nose burned from the cold so I pulled my cap entirely over my face.

"Are we having any fun yet?" This from Bill. No laughter.

Normally in tough situations this line draws some laughter and inspires one and all to cope. Bill's comment drew zero laughter and only a few soft groans, which seemed to take considerable effort. We were all rolled up in cocoons and had withdrawn to wage a private war with time and temperature.

At this moment on Kilimanjaro I developed a new definition of very cold. Very cold is when the temperature gets so low that even bitching about it requires too much effort.

Summit Day—Final Ascent, 15,400 Feet To The Top Of Africa

"Hello. It is time now. Please, it is time."

Felix Anasa Ocotu tapped lightly on our door and spoke softly. There was no need to speak loudly for we were all wide awake and suffering the cold.

David acknowledged our wake-up call in a bright, energetic voice. "Asante, Felix. It is time then, is it? Asante." And then to the frozen bodies in the stone hut, "It is ten past midnight, mates. Good morning to you and I trust you all slept well? Felix allowed us to sleep in an extra ten minutes."

"What a guy," responded the skeptical Bill Jackson.

Uniform groans emitted from the assembled, who had not slept well, if at all.

As I pulled myself out of the ice cold sleeping bag I prepared for the first test of the day. It is not uncommon to awake at high altitude to find yourself disoriented and depressed. I did a little psyche check and said the words, "Good morning, my friends." I was gratified that the words formed easily and were understood. I looked at faces and heard responses to my greeting from everyone on the team, so another test was passed.

In the uneven glow of bobbing flashlight beams I tried to observe the others, watching movements and listening for evidence of disorientation. Everyone seemed fine, no babbling nonsense, no serious withdrawl, no apparent motor problems. Cold, but fine.

I thought again of the climber we had met at Horombo Hut who had frightened his wife and teammates considerably by staggering about and speaking unintelligible sounds in this same shelter. No summit attempt for him.

We all dressed as quickly as numb hands and fingers would allow. Our shelter was so cold I could see my breath.

"Dress as warm as you can, mates for it will only become colder as we go up high." This from David.

My response: "Up high? Hell man, THIS IS up high." Small, feeble laughs from the assembled.

We all worked on building layers of clothing to retain body heat. Most of us put on heavy wool socks over poly liners. Then came polypropylene underwear, silk turtle neck, wool shirt and pants, a poly rain suit, down filled parka with fur lined hood and a knit poly watch cap. Most of us used synthetics and silk. The synthetics wick away moisture. Cotton soaks it up and keeps it, which is asking for trouble. No cotton on this ascent. Silk, I was surprised to learn, is a wonderful insulator. As the layers were added some of us began to look like the Michelin Man.

Kilimanjaro is a midnight ascent. Many people are surprised to learn that big mountains are often done at night, in the dark. It is particularly important on high snow fields and in ice chutes or when going up an open slope below rock formations. A final ascent in the early morning hours means that everything is frozen solid and stable. When the sun comes up, snow and ice can become slippery. As the thaw occurs rocks do break loose and tumble on down open slopes, acting much like very dangerous bowling balls. It is wise to climb in the dark, as challenging as it sounds, reach the summit and descend before the thaw. In late morning sunlight there are also several potential problems—sunburn, dehydration, and snow blindness. Because of the clarity of the air and reflections off snow and ice, the rays of the sun are wicked at high altitude.

Conventional wisdom would suggest climbing in daylight when the climber can see the mountain clearly and make beautiful photographs. So much for conventional wisdom. We will gladly forgo the view and the photographs for the safety of the dark and the cold. The best mountain expeditions, after all, *are* the ones you come back from.

Bill, The Friendly Pharmacist, came over and, groping about in the dark, found my arm, located my hand and pressed a Diamox tablet into my palm with a "don't drop it" message. I silently prayed that chemistry would help me get to the summit.

While there would be nothing to photograph until sunrise at the summit, I decided to pull out my Nikons for one last check. Normally I carry one Nikon 35mm with a 28mm wide angle lens. Weight is the issue in mountaineering and my Nikon, which is a lovely camera, was made with a metal case. It's heavy. Something made me bring along a backup, so I was carrying two Nikons and plenty of film. Extra weight, but Kili was a very special adventure and I didn't want to miss a single photo opportunity. Something told me I would only come this way once in my lifetime.

Felix dropped by to check on progress and distribute breakfast. The Tanzanians had done it again. Wood smoked hot tea.

Because of the nausea problems associated with high altitude, most of us opted to put little or nothing in our stomachs on the simple premise that what goes down will likely come up. I offered silent apologies to Issac Newton

I found my water bottle and swallowed a Diamox tablet. Imagine, Diamox for breakfast. Could I have it poached please with some Hollandaise, a pinch of dill and thyme and some Rusk toast. Maybe a slice of Canadian bacon. Diamox Benedict.

We stood in the dark all bundled up like a bunch of Wisconsin school kids on a winter day waiting for the school bell to ring. The atmosphere was somewhat like a locker room before the big game. Everyone was tense and excited and ready for the game to begin.

David broke the silence. "Remember, let's go slow, mates. Pole, pole. If Felix sets the pace too fast, let's slow it down. Pole, pole and we'll make it."

"All due respect, David, but I think it should be pole, pole, pole, pole, pole, pole . . . etcetera, etcetera." I said, going for the first real laugh of the day. No one laughed and a few people groaned.

David, ever the coach, continued, "Also remember the moon walk. As we get higher use the moon walk, it will help. And don't forget to cough periodically to clear your lungs. Very important."

The higher you go the harder it is for lungs to expel moisture. Coughing helps.

The moon walk is simply a process of locking the knee after each step. On a flat surface it seems awkward. But on a steep pitch the moon walk centers your weight and makes the next step much easier. While it makes for a slow, deliberate ascent, it also allows the legs to do the lifting. On a high mountain in very thin air, three or four steps at a time is sometimes all one can manage.

"Not to rush, mates, not to rush. Pole, pole," said the coach.

I thought about asking everyone to go out and win one for the Gipper, but my success as a comedian on this morning was marginal. And David was offering sound advice, best not to chide him.

We saw a moving light outside the meat locker. It was Felix, carrying an old fuel fired lantern, the kind railroad men once used. He stood and surveyed the team to see if everyone was fit to go.

It was a great scene. Six climbers in arctic parkas gathered around a native guide who was holding an old lantern. The flame flickered and danced in the coal black shelter. The lantern had once been shiny brass. It now had a dull patina and the lantern glass was smudged here and there with soot. The smell of burning kerosene caused noses to wrinkle. There was a tantalizing wave of heat now and then as Felix moved the lantern to look each of us in the eye, to read our faces, to learn of any complications before the final challenge began.

I looked into his eyes. The whites shined in contrast to his dark brown, smooth, calm face. He was expressionless. The old lantern cast his shadow on the stone wall.

Felix looked like someone in a Jack London novel. His brown face was framed by an orange wool hood. His parka was old and worn. His wool pants were tucked into his boots and orange wool socks came up over his calfs effecting a knicker-like style. His boots were almost identical to mine—heavy lug soles, ankle high, reinforced toe, heavy leather, dark from sealing wax and mountain dirt . . . and red laces.

I smiled at the red laces. I always put red laces in my mountain boots. A touch of color for the man who dresses with a little flair. Also helpful in identifying remains, should there be any.

I'm wearing boots just like the African pros, I thought. Except my boots are shaking a little.

"We go now," said Felix The Understated. "We go slow and steady in single line. Pole, pole."

And a voice, which sounded very much like mine, said, "No Felix."

He looked at me with surprise.

"We go pole, pole, pole, pole, pole, ecetera, etcetera."

Felix actually laughed at my attempt at Swahili humor. My colleagues also laughed, although I think it was at me rather than with me.

"OK, we go."

Outside the shelter two other figures emerged from the dark. Felix introduced his assistant guides who had been all but invisible on the trek to base camp.

"This assistant guide Josef, this assistant guide Goodluck."

Both men smiled in the lantern light and nodded their heads. They were young, but had a studied look about them that indicated they had done this before and were very much at home on this monster mountain at 12:30 AM.

Josef, at 5'8", looked much like Felix and was dressed in a parka, blue jeans and mountain boots. Goodluck was slight, perhaps 5'4" or so, and wore a faded one-piece orange jump suit, much like the suit one would wear sky-diving. It offered good protection against the wind and was billowing even now, catching the wind as gusts occurred at regular intervals. An orange knit hat completed Goodluck's outfit. As he moved, I noticed he swaggered a bit. He seemed entirely confident. We did not.

Goodluck, clearly the more animated of the three guides, sported a wiry goatee on his chin, unusual I thought in this part of Africa. Our guide's clothing looked more western than African. But then I realized that these natives spent a great deal of time with people from all parts of the world. They have been exposed to countless cultures and styles and would undoubtedly pick up the good and the bad.

We waited in the dark for Felix to begin the ascent. I spoke with Joseph and Goodluck and told them how much we appreciated their help and their skill. They were pleasant, polite, soft spoken and ready to help us to the summit. Moments later I mentioned this friendly quality to Bill. "Guess they haven't climbed with the French," he cracked.

Felix appeared, his lantern smoking and swinging gently with the rhythm of his stride. Even at this altitude he moved with grace. Bruno, Frankie and Bill moved up the line into lead positions. Dwight, David, and Patrick would bring up the rear. Josef and Goodluck took flank positions. We took our first steps toward the summit at 12:40 AM. It was an exciting moment.

The night was the very definition of black. India ink black. Darker than a Russian depression.

In America we spend most of our lives in urban somewhere. Even in the most remote rural setting, the smallest town or village, there will be a light. A yard light, a barn light, the passing headlights of a car or truck, the blue light of a television, the blinking lights of an aircraft overhead, the glow of city lights on the horizon, a beer sign in the window of the neighborhood tavern—there will be light. At 15,400 feet on Kilimanjaro in East Africa there was no light, no point of reference, no light offering proof of life.

Felix fired up his lantern and this became our beacon, the only light we would need. And it swayed with his every step, almost like a metronome, keeping us on the beat, on the step.

It is against my nature to blindly follow anything or anyone. I've challenged authority all my life. I've challenged ideas, ideals and the direction, integrity and intent of the leadership I've encountered. But this night I choose to follow. I put my faith in a quiet African named Felix, a man I had known for less than four days. I sensed in him the quiet resolve, the patience and self-confidence that good leaders always seem to have.

Throughout the long, slow, deliberate trek to base camp, Felix was always at the end of our line, making sure all were well, making certain that no one got far behind or developed problems on the trail. Tonight he was the leader, he was the point man. I could not actually see him in the dark. I could see a glow from his swinging lantern, the occasional shadow, and the persistent motion that said "follow me."

At times like this it is perfectly normal to question one's judgment. What on earth was I doing in this high place? I found myself asking and answering this question on Kili with some frequency. The answer is always the same. Some of us require a greater degree of risk than others. Some of us require risk to remind ourselves that we are alive and capable of much more than we ever dreamed.

At an early age I decided to put myself at risk, to walk along the edge, to take the difficult and uncertain path on a regular basis. In so doing I've found that I acquire a broader, clearer view, intellectually, emotionally and spiritually, of the world around me and life in general. I have been careful to accept risks with fallback positions, with some type of alternative or net. In sky diving, for example, there are two parachutes, a main and a reserve. This attempt on Kilimanjaro had a fallback position. One can always decide to abandon the quest for the top and simply come down, down to the safety and security of oxygen rich air at lower altitudes and moderate temperatures. If the going got too tough, I thought, I will simply throw in the towel and head down the mountain. And another voice, the alter ego voice said, "Not without a fight, buddy."

Except for the swinging lantern I had no point of reference but the body in front of me. It was a case of simply following the elephant in front of you, just like in the circus. If there was a trail I couldn't see it. If there was a slope I couldn't feel it. It was simply too dark to see anything.

A wonderful Groucho Marx line emerged from some distant recess in my brain: "Outside of a dog a book is man's best friend. Inside of a dog it is simply too dark to read."

For the first thirty minutes the pitch was very gradual and the terrain seemed almost flat at times. Where is this steep pitch to the summit I had heard so much about? And suddenly the pitch changed. It was like walking in a dark room and suddenly hitting a wall. David broke the silence. "Up we go mates, here it is. Pole, pole."

The change in pitch was so sever I actually stumbled forward and put out a hand to cushion what I though was going to be a fall. I planted my hiking stick and began digging my toes into the mountain and up I went.

Each breath now became a deliberate effort. The heavy feeling of exertion, so familiar in mountaineering now began in my chest.

The pace seemed a bit fast and after a time I noticed that Felix wasn't pausing to rest, just pressing on. Most guides, however thoughtful, make this mistake. For all their empathy they simply take for granted their conditioning, age (they are almost always younger) and their acclimatization. It is natural for them to move more quickly and more persistently.

We would be moving up this steep pitch for at least six hours. How, I wondered, could we maintain this pace?

I looked for a bucket of resolve, a light weight bucket, planted my iron tipped Kilimajaro stick and continued the step, step, step following the swinging lantern light.

Any glamour associated with mountain climbing disappears rather quickly when you hit a severe pitch at high altitude. The trek can be monotonous and punishing. It is very hard work.

When people hear the phrase "mountain climbing" the popular image is one of a brightly dressed climber with a climbing helmet, dark glasses, boots with crampons (metal spikes), dangling from a multi-colored nine millimeter mountain rope over some alpine valley thousands of death defying feet below. He is usually smiling.

It is a vision in living color on the pages of National Geographic, in a PBS television documentary or on the cover of numerous glossy magazines that glamorize outdoor adventure.

At every opportunity I try to correct that image or at least balance it a bit. Most mountaineering is not as colorful or macho. It is the stuff of one foot in front of the other and sometimes one hand hold before the other, for hours at a time. It may come as a shock to the uninitiated, but climbing the highest mountain on earth, Mt. Everest, is mostly putting one foot in front of the other for many days. It has been called the longest "walk up" on earth.

I have enormous respect for those who tackle the sheer faces of some of the world's most difficult mountains. On these technical ascents a climber must use every skill and every climbing device or tool in the book to reach the summit. Their courage, strength of body and mind and their stamina is incredible.

In learning the ropes (a phrase which is almost literal in mountaineering) I have put on a climbing harness, chalked my hands to improve grip, and climbed up a nearly sheer rock face. The first time my heart nearly pounded out of my chest, muscles twitched in stress and fear, and I discovered the smell of a rock as I gripped the granite in front of me with everything I had, including my nose.

I've been to school on rock climbing, snow and ice climbing and other techniques to become familiar with the skills, just in case. I have also dangled in the air on a rope, a couple of times in 25 years of mountaineering, both times in practice, for what might come. It is dramatic and thrilling. But most climbing is not dramatic. Picking one's way up mountain slopes and through rock fields above 15,000 feet, hour after hour, day after day does not make for dramatic pictures or exciting video.

But frankly, I much prefer to keep both feet on the ground and then go as high as my will and the mountain will allow.

Step, step, step, step. Breathe in, push air out, remind yourself to cough every now and then, move one foot in front of the other, believe the summit can be achieved, then reach into the recesses of your mind and try to find some motivation.

Climbing in the dark presents a disadvantage which is not exactly obvious. I have found that one must work much harder at self-motivation. In daylight mountains can be pure magic. The views dazzle and delight, the sight of the summit releases adrenalin and the sheer beauty of the high landscape or the valleys below provides an incredible boost for the psyche and an elixer for the heart that deadens pain and offers promise.

In the dark the muscles can handle the pain of a climb, but the mind can take a real beating. At night it is almost impossible to see progress. Without some sense of progress fatigue and depression can amplify the physical pain and make it devilishly hard for a mountaineer to continue.

My thoughts turned to my indefatigable friend, Robb Mitchell, who is moving even when he's sitting still. Once again, I recall the message on one of his favorite t-shirts: "The higher I get, the higher I get." What incredible spirit. But it is hard to get high when you can't see where you're going, where you have been or any indication of progress.

In this dark hour I miss the warm reassurance of the sun.

Step, step, step, step, breath deeply, cough, push it out. Step, step, step, step.

I stumble in the dark, thump against a rock, scrape the skin on my hand attempting to break a fall. There is that momentary sickening feeling when you lose your footing and experience an unexpected fall. I put my face in the gravel of Kilimanjaro. In the dark it was a kiss I didn't even seen coming. And I always see a kiss coming. I like to kiss. Gravel? No. I'm up in a scramble. Nothing major. All part of the deal. I dust off and quick step to make up for the four or five steps I've lost. Coordination problem? Altitude sickness? No. Just clumsy. So, push on and fight the monotony of the dark ascent.

Our group is in a typical switchback route, one that zig zags from side to side making the ascent much easier and challenging the old notion that a straight line is the shortest distance between two points. A straight line ascent up a pitch this steep would be futile.

Suddenly the lantern light stops swinging and the procession comes to a halt. A rest stop. How wonderful. Why didn't we think of this sooner? Imagine. Resting. Allowing the body to recover. What a helluva great idea. It is the first rest stop in over an hour. All remain silent, all take on water and all, no doubt, are thinking, "Damn, five more hours of this. Can I do it?"

The lantern begins swinging again. Felix The Unrelenting is doing his best imitation of an Army drill sergeant. Up we go.

I'm reminded of a drill sergeant I followed in Army infantry training. His name was Sgt. Albert King. He was short and thick, a tad overweight. He smoked cigars and drank a lot of beer. He was much older than we green trainees and had a few Korean War battle wounds as well, but he marched us into the ground, without perspiring. We hated him, but the hate kept us focused and moving, just as he knew it would. He was the best.

Sgt. Felix pressed onward and upward and his troops followed in the dark.

I began to notice the weight of my camera pack. It was a light load, a piece of angel food cake. But my light pack was beginning to get heavy. Not a real good sign.

At 15,000 feet the atmosphere provides only 50% of the oxygen available at sea level. We were now at least 1500 feet higher, perhaps 16,500, more than three miles into the sky.

I bumped into Dwight. The line had come to a sudden stop. Assistant guide Goodluck Christopher scrambled past me in the dark. There was a commotion up ahead, the lantern was not swinging. Something's up.

Frankie Spite was doubled up with one knee on the ground. Goodluck was behind her with his arms around her waist, pulling her up. Frankie was tossing her cookies. Up came tea and breakfast. Altitude sickness was taking its toll.

"Altitude check. Anyone know how high we are. Anyone have a clue?"

"Maybe sixteen five," someone mumbled.

It was very quiet. Only small expressions of encouragement for Frankie could be heard. Silence. Not like our group at all. Lethargy had arrived. The silence was another indication that everyone was suffering and fighting personal battles with the atmosphere. Slight depression had set in. Talking required effort.

Frankie's problem gave us an opportunity to rest. Even in the yellow lantern light she seemed pale. But she looked up, smiled somehow and indicated she was ready to push on.

You had to admire her pluck. As she shouldered her pack, I wondered how many of the men on this mountain would give up and go down as long as she was on her feet, moving ahead.

I caught David by the arm. "Game lady, David. I do believe that if Frankie makes it to the summit every guy in this group will make it to the summit. What's the bet?"

He looked at me for a moment with a question in his eye, then smiled and said, "No bet, mate, it's true."

Slow deliberate paces now. Step, step, step, step. Breathe deeply, cough, let the lungs work. Then step, step, step, step.

I concentrated on where the climber in front of me put his feet. I tried to follow in his footsteps, tried to stay close to him, let him set the pace. It was very hard work.

My recurring image of the night was the classic circus ring elephant parade. Each elephant grasped the tail of the elephant in front and followed the big butt around the ring. But where was the cheering crowd? Where was the encouragement? Where was the motivation? If the crowd could see this procession, I thought, they wouldn't cheer, they would have us committed. I recalled the tongue-in-cheek question in the pub in Scotland, "You'll be telling us which hospital you're from, lad, we'll be taken' you back now."

The switchbacks were tighter now and more frequent. The pitch was great and becoming greater. I could actually reach out with my left hand and steady myself on the rock slope. On my right, the downhill side, it was inky black and windy. I went through a mental drill—Pat, if you slip, lean to the left and grab.

We continued the pace, step, step, step, step. Our heads were down, mind and body concentrating on every single step, drawn like insects to the swinging lantern up ahead. Sgt. Felix was leading us to the summit.

I caught sight of Bill just briefly. The lantern light caught his expression, a look I had come to know. His face said, "We've come this far and we are not giving up now." Clearly the competitive athlete in him was at work, moving him forward.

My right hand began to ache. At first I thought it was the cold. I switched the hiking stick to my left hand and then realized the pain was the result of a death grip I had been applying. With relaxation came circulation. I grasped the stick firmly but relaxed my grip between steps.

Then came a slip and I went down on one knee, grasping rock with one hand. My knee jammed into sharp rock and the pain was significant. Goodluck was on the job and arrested my slide from behind. I crouched against the mountain and felt a kind of sinking feeling. I'm running out of gas, I thought. Goodluck tugged on the strap of my pack.

"Give to me," he whispered, tugging gently. I grabbed his hand and struggled into a standing position, wobbling back and forth in the wind.

"No chance, my friend, it's my pack and I'll carry it. I'm OK."

No expression from the native guide. He simply pointed ahead and said, "We go." And we went. I resolved I would carry my pack to the summit.

By now our group was separating. The stronger climbers moved ahead. Bill was doing very well and was up front with David Schrock and Bruno. Germans are tough. Bruno had told us so. Felix and his swinging lantern was out of sight and several hundred feet above my position. I was dead last and losing ground to the rest of the team.

I began to look for some way to self-motivate and decided to count steps. I decided I would take ten steps and rest, allowing my breathing to stabilize and then take ten more steps. In this pattern I would find some rhythm.

One, two, three, four, five, six, seven, eight nine and . . . ten. Stop. Lean left into the mountain, let the mountain hold me up, suck in air, cough, suck in air and blow it out, clear the lungs, wait for the pounding in the chest to diminish and then take . . . ten more steps. It was a classic carrot and stick approach. The carrot was the rest stop after the tenth step. I was the stick. The carrot always won. Goodluck caught on to my routine and we continued up the mountain in the dark for over an hour. Ten steps at a time.

How long is an hour in the dark? Life this night was measured in heart beats and footsteps. The eyes cannot see progress, the inner clock cannot track the time. Steps, ten to twelve inches in length, felt like a heroic achievement at times. Minutes could not be registered, but seconds were counted by the heartbeat in my ears. Thump ka thump, thump ka thump, thump ka thump. Ten. Rest. Lean. Cough. Breathe. Over and over and over again.

The mind wanders to sports. I try distracting myself by counting all the sports I've played in my life—football, basketball, baseball and tennis during the school years. Ah, yes, also bowling, hockey, and badminton. Later in life I played quarterback in city league football in Wisconsin and had to quit smoking to do it.

Nasty habit, smoking. Picked it up in the Army—cigarettes, cigars and pipes—man, I was a triple threat smoker. The first day of football practice I discovered I couldn't wheeze my way through a practice, much less be effective in a game. The choice was either football or smoking. So, I quit cold-turkey at age 27 and never looked back.

I continued to put one foot in front of the other. Can you smoke and climb mountains successfully? Stay tuned.

Let's see, I have down hill skied in Wisconsin, Colorado and Utah, cross country skied in the forests of northern Wisconsin, hit the elusive golf ball, and pounded the volleyball and the racquetball. Do horseshoes and croquet count?

Since moving to Memphis I've played goal keeper on two soccer teams. Never played cricket. Did thirty minutes of rugby once and gave blood. Did manage to jump out of a perfectly good airplane at 3,500 feet and executed a three point landing without knocking my lights out. Actually did this more than once. Is sky diving a sport? But why jump out of a perfectly good airplane?

Did try La Crosse and found it exciting. I wonder if the Indians actually played with a human skull in place of the ball? Ran a few ten K's. Is distance running a sport? Or is it masochism? No, it's a sport. Is biking a sport? Does Lance Armstrong wear yellow jerseys? 'Have paddled many canoe miles down some beautiful rivers. Never up river, always down, which proves I have an IQ higher than 65. Have bungee jumped. Once was enough. Bungee jumping is not a sport. I've been blessed, I deducted, with better than average coordination and good reflexes, unless I've been out with that rogue Johnny Walker or on the road to Bombay.

The distraction of counting sports ceased when I began slipping and stumbling with some regularity on Kili. I blamed it on the dark, on the scree, on the mountain gremlins guarding the summit. Couldn't be me, said he.

One of the most sickening feelings in life is to have the wind knocked out of your body. Everything seems to stop. Nothing seems to be working. You feel as if you are choking. Your mind tells the body to breath and the body says, "Invalid command, invalid command." You cannot speak. You cannot even muster a respectable gasp. Or a cry for help.

And then, after an interminable wait of about five years, a bit of air breaks through and the chest begins to move and blue turns to red, red becomes yellow, yellow becomes embarrassment, and you're back to red again.

The fall knocked the stuffing out of me. There was nothing to do but wait for some air to return and there was damned little air above 17,000 feet.

At first I thought I was slipping and then the mountain jumped up and hit me in the back. Out went the air and the fun began.

Goodluck pulled my belt trying to get everything in the diaphram working again. Finally I was able to sit and with his help, stand, but I knew I was in real trouble.

When Goodluck loosened the straps on my pack and removed it he got no protest from me. I was whipped. What fine madness this is, I thought. I'm so beat I can't even keep my feet under me. The summit is only 1500 feet away, but it might as well be 1500 miles away.

I leaned into the mountain, felt the cold rock on my face and just concentrated on breathing. I actually had to think about breathing. How did that go again? In, out, in out? I finally hunched down into a sitting position and closed my eyes.

"Come, Patrick, come." It was Goodluck pulling on my arm. I don't know how long I had been out, perhaps only a few minutes, but I felt as if I had awaken from a long nap. My mind seemed compressed. Goodluck was patiently attempting to get me up and moving again, not down, but up. "Come. Come. Not far."

The diminutive assistant guide was encouraging me to continue. So, I stood up, took a deep breath and started moving forward once again. Ten paces at a time.

My coordination was terrible. Muscles were not getting enough oxygen, the brain was not working well. I had an out of body conversation with the organ team. "C'mon guys," I said to the red cells, "pump a little more oxygen to the muscles, don't let me down now. Another hour or so and we'll make the summit." They answered.

> "What's wrong with you, Mages? If you would take us where we can get some oxygen we will be glad to pump the muscles up. That's our job, dummy. But when we took this assignment Mother Nature promised us a decent supply of oxygen. Your model wasn't designed to go this high. You keep abusing us and we will quit. At the moment we have banned together and organized a work slow-down. It's just a warning. Keep this up and we'll form a union. Yeah, that's it. We'll unite, form a union and shut you down faster than you can say 'arbitration.' And we'll organize the white cells too. So, don't screw with us. Take us down the hill."

Go down the hill? There it was. The first hint of defeat, the first suggestion of "quit." Grey matter was actually producing the most negative of negative thoughts: go down. My psyche had put retreat on the table.

Goodluck rescued me. "Come, we go. Pole, pole." There was no "give up" in Mr. Christopher. He left his position behind me and moved ahead. He stood about two feet in front of me facing up the mountain and showing me his back. He directed my right hand to his shoulder and without any conversation made his intent very clear. He would lead, I would follow. Together we would continue up Kilimanjaro.

At first it was shaky and difficult to keep my hand on his shoulder. But soon we developed a kind of rhythm. We began taking five steps together. I would match his steps while holding onto his right shoulder. It was the strong, wiry Wachagga native, leading the punch drunk American, the sighted leading the blind. Touching him was a useful approach. We moved on, just five steps at a time.

Whenever I needed a break I simply squeezed his shoulder. I noted that it took longer to regain control of my breathing each time we stopped. Stops were frequent. My chest would be heaving like a runner at the end of a one hundred yard dash. There were times when I thought I would never get it under control. In those moments I experienced a temporary panic which was then followed by some soft cursing and more gasping. I decided not to lean against the mountain or sit during the breaks. If I sat down I doubted I would have the stuff to get up again. The climb would be over.

Felix, his swinging lantern and the rest of the team were now so far above us we could not see even a faint glow. Bill later told me that all were moving very, very slowly, but they were moving. "I had it down to about six steps at a time," Bill reported. "I got into a six step rhythm. We were like a bunch of cows behind a bell cow, just following the lead cow, remaining silent and just working out our own individual motivation. I kept telling myself, no matter how much it hurt, that I had come this far and refused to quit at this point, although quit had entered my mind more than once."

Goodluck took my arm and put it on his shoulder and we plodded on, five steps at a time, then rest, then five more steps. The process hurt, it really hurt. But we continued.

Step.

Step.

Step.

Step.

Step.

Stop, bend over, breath deeply, suck in air, cough, make the lungs work, cough again, get the heaving chest under control. And then Goodluck would say, "Come, we go."

Step.

Step.

Step.

Step.

Step.

At this point I knew that without Goodluck I wouldn't have a chance at reaching the summit. His patience was incredible. He knew I was in trouble, but he would keep on as long as I could stand. I wondered if I could do Kilimanjaro on my hands and knees?

I was doing everything I could to self-motivate, but I desperately wanted to throw in the towel, to signal the referee the fight was over.

And then Goodluck began to sing.

I had heard stories about the guides and porters singing to pass the time on long passages to the summit. They often sing hymns taught by missionaries and simple native songs which almost become chants.

Goodluck's voice was soft, almost child-like.

"Kili, Kili, Kila

Kila-man-jar-oh,

Kili, Kili, Kila

Kila-man-jar-oh . . . "

It was a simple melody, rather sing-song in quality. At a lower altitude, I thought, one could step on each word with two steps on the word Kilaman-jaro. At this altitude that pace was out of the question.

Just when I thought I couldn't take another step, Goodluck would sing . . . .

"Kili, Kili, Kila,

Kila-man-jar-oh."

And I would reach down into my dwindling bucket of resolve and find a few more steps.

On the next break I noted that the sky was beginning to lighten. The sun was working its way around the world and beginning to reach Africa once again.

Goodluck shook my arm. I protested. "Sorry, Goodluck, not yet."

He shook me again and when I opened my eyes he was trying to hand me a Nikon from my camera pack. "Look, look. Take picture."

Making photographs, normally my passion, was the furthest thing from my mind. But he was right, this was a Kodak moment. The growing light revealed a sea of boiling clouds below us. The scene looked like a witches cauldron of bubbling spirits, an angry ocean, rolling and boiling. This ethereal scene was punctuated by a small sun flair on the horizon below us.

Instinctively I raised the camera and flipped the film advance lever to activate the light meter. What exposure? The light meter was no use in a situation like this. Think, buddy. What exposure? My mind was mush. So, I simply opened up the 28mm lens all the way and dialed a slow shutter speed. I don't know which speed I selected but when I pushed the shutter release it sounded like a fourth of a second, perhaps a half second. I made one exposure and handed the camera to Goodluck. No bracketing, no back up frame, just one click. It's all I could do.

I had learned photography at a young age from two fine professionals, Robert Kenneth Geisel and Joseph Kerestessy. The Geisel Studio was an industrial/commercial business and Bob was an artist, teacher and man of the world in every sense.

Bob Geisel taught me how to see. Joe, a Hungarian immigrant, taught me the rudiments of making pictures, both with the camera and in the darkroom. One principle I learned very quickly at the hands of these two masters—to make one good image you must first make several images. On this night, a night when breathing was a major challenge, I violated the principle, I made only one exposure. The pain and exhaustion were simply too great.

And then I remembered the pithy and accurate Vince Lombardi deduction: "Fatigue makes cowards of us all."

Once again, Goodluck woke me from my standing state of depression and said, "Come, we go." I reached out for his shoulder and prepared to take another five steps.

Step.

Step.

Step.

Step.

That's all. Just four this time. Four was the best I could do. Down to four, I thought. Fading fast. I dreamed of Otis elevators. I dreamed of escalators and chair lifts.

But Goodluck pushed ahead . . . and somehow I followed.

We had been climbing for almost six hours. It was now very bright and for the first time I could actually see the mountain. Facing us and much above us was a large boulder field with huge chunks of lava rising up like a wall. The only way to the top was over or through the wall. My stomach suddenly felt very empty. I shivered two or three times and it had nothing to do with the cold wind. The journey ahead looked formidable.

The sun was up and provided a brief psychological boost. The view, however, was depressing. No sign of the summit. No sign of my fellow climbers. Just rock and sky.

Goodluck pressed on, four steps at a time.

I thought I head a sound, a voice. I squeezed Goodluck's shoulder and we stopped so the crunching noise from boot on rock would not interfere. We listened. There it was, a shout from above, followed by another shout. Goodluck turned and smiled. "They are on summit."

All I could think to say was my favorite exclamation, "Wow!" All Goodluck could think was, "Let's go."

"Come, Patrick. You make it." We moved ahead, four steps at a time.

At one rest stop I strained to see the summit. No summit in sight. I looked down the mountain and the view was magnificent. The mountain fell away and seemed to go down forever. I then rested my chin on my chest and concentrated on breathing.

Goodluck touched my arm and said, "Look." As I looked down the mountain I noticed some movement. Goodluck pointed to my far right. Something was moving across our field of vision and very much below us. I struggled to comprehend. What is it? Suddenly there was a glimmer of sun and something shiny was moving from right to left. Slowly, out of the darkness, emerged a beautiful bird heading south with small red eyes blinking at us. It was at least two thousand feet below us. On its tail was the Union Jack flag, the livery of British Airways. The bird was a Boeing, a large commercial jet aircraft, looking just like a small desk top model or an ornament you might hang on a Christmas tree. It was flying below us. We were higher in the sky than a very large airplane.

Goodluck tugged on my arm and we moved on once again.

Step.

Step.

Step.

That's it. I was now down to three steps and many minutes of gasping to re-gain control. Three steps. How long, I wondered, could I continue? And why am I on this mountain? This IS madness and I'm the Mad Hatter. Oh, to find the magic rabbit hole. Certainly the rabbit hole would go down. Alice did.

What did Britain's number one lion say, when things were tough? Winston Spencer Churchill, the greatest leader of the 20ᵗʰ Century, excelled at motivation. Churchill's biography could consist of one line, his line, "Never give up, never give up, never give up." He rallied an entire Island nation and made them believe they would defend their homeland successfully and win the Great War, in spite of being out gunned and out manned. His message to Germany, "We will never give up."

That's it, I thought. I will do one step for each of Churchill's words, "Never give up."

Step. "Never."

Step. "Give."

Step. "Up."

Rest. Restore breathing. Cough, clear the lungs. Then step up the mountain.

Step. "Never."

Step. "Give."

Step. "Up."

For the past hour I had been using the moon walk technique, locking one knee before taking the next step up, allowing the stronger leg muscles to do the work. Step, lock knee, shift weight, step, lock the other knee, shift weight, step. I was moving very slowly, hand on Goodluck's shoulder, but I was still moving.

The ever present gnawing question, "How much further to the summit?" Impossible to tell. The pitch on Kili is so steep I could not see the top. We must be close, I thought. It was as much a plea as it was an observation.

A queezy feeling began building in my stomach. It wasn't nausea, which I expected. Some climbers toss up everything but the stomach when altitude sickness really takes hold. The queezy feeling was anxiety, just before actual fear.

I was playing tag on the playground of Franklin elementary school in Wausau, Wisconsin. A fourth grade classmate who was "it" singled me out and the chase was on. I began to run and soon realized "it" was gaining on me and tag was inevitable. The queezy feeling of eminent capture started in my brain and dropped to my stomach. The more I struggled to run the lower the feeling went. Soon it was in my knees and then my legs turned to Jello. No matter how much I wanted to run, the queez of anxiety sapped my strength and I soon felt the thump of the tag and the scream of my classmates. I had failed to elude and now I was "it."

Easy does it, Patrick. There is no chase. This is not a contest. Take your time. Shake off anxiety. There is no time limit. Just run your own race and you will make it. All these thoughts brought some comfort and I continued the continuum, the endless series of slow, deliberate steps, three at a time.

Step. "Never."

Step. "Give."

Damn, I'm down to two steps. Two is all I can do. I can't get the "Up" step, the third step. Aww, Winston, you could have simply said, "Don't quit."

I squeezed Goodluck's shoulder and we stopped. Now I was actually counting the number of breaths it took to recover. It was two steps up, pause, rest and count 16 breaths to get past the gasping and heaving of the chest. What splendid madness, leaning against a mountain somewhere above 18,000 feet in the sky and counting breaths.

The sun was now very bright. I fished out my glacier glasses, very dark glasses designed to cope with the UV rays and reflection one encounters on a high mountain. It is possible, I reminded myself, to sun burn the whites of the eyes. I had experienced this on a glacier and it feels like you have sand in your eyes. Sun usually lifts the spirits but on this day it did very little to lift anything in me. It was now all about motivation, finding the resolve to continue, when most of the fibers in your body are saying, quit.

During the six hours of ascent through the night I had often recited poetry or lyrics. I spoke the lines of Langston Hughes, Robert Frost, Robert Burns and a few I had written myself. It's always nice for a would-be poet to place himself in the good company of real poets. I even quoted a bit of ancient Greek wisdom and noted that there was very little modern Greek wisdom to quote. Had the Greeks used up all their wisdom? Or was it the Uzo or Retsina?

Step. "Don't."

Step. "Quit."

Pause. Count sixteen breaths. And move up.

Step. "Don't."

Step. "Quit."

When Bobby Kennedy was on the stump for the Presidency he was often asked why a millionaire, who could sit on his butt and deposit dividend checks, was subjecting himself to the wrenching task of running for the highest office in the land. He would look down at scuffed shoes, roll up his wrinkled shirt sleeves, push a lock of hair off his forehead and quote Aeschylus, "Men are not made for safe havens."

Step. "Don't"

Step. "Quit."

Pause. Count sixteen breaths and move up.

Commander Grace Hopper, later Admiral Hopper, was the Navy computer expert who co-authored Cobal, an enduring computer language. The Navy had retired her twice and both times the computers went to hell and they brought her back. When asked why she continued to come out of retirement and chase Navy computer problems she spoke of Naval vessels. "Ships in port are safe. But that's not what ships are built for."

Step. "Don't"

Step. "Quit."

Pause. Count sixteen breaths. No, make that seventeen, maybe eighteen.

I tried Frost. What was the name of the poem? I couldn't bring it up. The old gray computer was not working. What were the lines?

"The woods are cold and deep?" No, "The woods are cold and dark and deep." That's it. "Going home on a snowy night," or something like that.

"The woods are cold and dark and deep,

But I have promises to keep,

And miles to go before I sleep.

And miles to go before I sleep."

Step.

Step.

Pause. Don't quit. Count eighteen breaths and keep your promises. Get the summit. Do not give up.

My mind called up the memory of a 14,000 foot summit in Colorado. I sat against a rock with my tent wrapped around me to provide protection from the wind. I was on a snow field, dead tired, in desperate need of rest. I had miscalculated the advancing weather and was trying to decide whether to pitch the tent and ride out the weather, retrace my steps and go down to a safer position, or to push up and over the mountain to the shelter of the eastern slope. None of the options appealed to me. Sleep appealed to me. Warmth appealed to me. A warm beer really appealed to me.

I opted to move ahead to the safer position on the eastern slope. It took a very difficult hour wading through knee deep snow to reach the shelter of a boulder field. I quickly pitched my tent and crawled into a sleeping bag and was soon warm, safe and sleeping like a child. When I woke up I replayed the events, which could have gone very wrong and then created several lines which I scribbled on a damp copy of a White River Forest map.

> "Mountains are very unforgiving,
> If your only goal is living.
> If you life is challenge, then,
> Pick up your pack and climb again."

Step.

Step.

Pause. Eighteen breaths, maybe nineteen or twenty. Shake off the pain. Move up. Do not give up. Don't quit. Climb again.

I leaned on Goodluck Christopher, who smiled and moved ahead, patiently allowing me to stumble after him. Goodluck was tired and he relished the rest stops with me. But he never wavered. Quit was not in him.

Step.

Step.

Lock knee.

Another step. Lock knee

Pause. Count eighteen, no twenty-four breaths. Deep breaths.

Squeeze Goodluck's shoulder and move up.

Where in the hell is the top of this god-almighty mountain?

And the mountain said, "It's here."

The Summit Of Kilimanjaro—Reaching The Top Of Africa

My head was bowed, chin on chest. I was holding Goodluck's shoulder with one hand and leaning against the mountain. He was pointing. "Come, Patrick."

The summit was not more than 20 steps away. Tears came fast. I wiped them away. 'Couldn't have my native climbing partner see the tears. Real men don't cry.

Give it a second thought, Patrick . . . of course they do.

I could see Bill. He was sitting in the sun with his hat off and his eyes closed, leaning against a lava boulder.

Step.

Step.

Step.

Step.

Don't rush it. Pole, pole. Don't rush it. Pause, rest. Step up. I pulled myself up one last boulder and I was standing on the summit, the highest point on the Continent of African. We were higher than anyone from the shores of the Mediteranean to the Cape Of Good Hope. Higher than millions of people. Higher than I had ever been in my life.

David was laying on a rock and appeared exhausted. His right arm was folded over his eyes. No one was moving. All were silent.

Frankie was sitting with her knees pulled up, arms wrapped around her legs, resting her head on her knees. She looked like an Andrew Wyeth painting—young woman dreaming on the top of a continent.

Dwight sat on a rock with his back against the mountain, staring vacantly. Bruno was nearby sitting with his legs spread before him, hands in his lap, holding his glasses, head back, eyes closed as if sunning himself at the seashore. A seashore, no doubt invented by Germans, conquered first by Germans, who also won the international sand castle contest while writing opera and beating everyone at soccer.

The guides were also silent. They sat in a group, huddled against the cold.

Just fifteen paces away I could see the actual summit point. A small white flag whipped in the wind. It was tattered.

I looked for a place to sit and moved toward it. The last few steps were like wading through waist deep water. I tried to sit down, lost all control and fell to the ground. I propped myself up, drew my knees to my chest and rested my head on my knees.

I heard some hand clapping and looked up. Goodluck and David were clapping and looking at me with smiles. Soon others took up the clapping and tears welled up once again. I was the last on the summit. But I was there.

"Good show, mate. You made it now, didn't you? Good show, real grit. Let me see your face, how are you?"

I reluctantly looked up, tears running down the stubble of a four day beard.

"You're white, pale, how do you feel?"

"It hurts," was all I could manage.

"Well, you paid for it mate, but you made it. Well done."

I put my head down again and let the tears run off my nose. It was one of the happiest moments of my life.

Bill came over and began pulling cameras out of my pack. He stepped back with one of my Nikons and began taking pictures of the group. He was moving around quite well and appeared to be in good shape. Oh to be 33 again, I thought.

He took some pictures of the author in a state of collapse. What I didn't know, and the real cause of his photographic zeal, was the unreal contrast he saw. I looked like death warmed over and was fighting to get as much oxygen as I could. Our guide, Felix The Amazing, was sitting next to me, puffing on a cigarette.

After sitting motionless for about ten minutes I began to feel better. Everyone began to move around, taking in the extraordinary view of the Kilimajaro volcano crater six hundred to seven hundred feet deep. It was time to get summit pictures.

Even the small motions required to pull out cameras was enough to drive away the good feelings I was having. I sat down again to gain some strength.

The highest point at our location on the rim of the volcano was a massive lava boulder. Talking in sign language and hand signals I got Bill to move up to the flag. He stood up and removed the hood of his parka. He spread his feet to find a balance point and gave the compulsory wave of the conqueror. I made several pictures, bracketing carefully. He then sat down and stretched out on the rock, exhausted but victorious. At this point in his life, Bill was the ultimate competitor and this was the sweetest victory of his mountaineering career.

"Your turn, big guy, get your butt up there."

I was feeling terrible again. "Can't do it, William."

"Get up there. You busted your ass and we will have a summit shot."

Bill handed me a t-shirt he had designed. The back said, "Mt. Kilimanjaro." The front said, "19,380 feet." I appreciate the trophy now, but on summit day I could have cared less. I didn't have the energy to put it on.

Goodluck Christopher and his right shoulder were never very far away. As I wobbled toward the summit rock he steadied me until I was in position for the obligatory summit photo and then moved away. It was to be the conquering hero shot, white hunter bags big mountain, and not a Hemingway in sight.

I caught Goodluck's arm and pulled him toward me. He protested, but my grip convinced him he was needed.

"No way, my friend, come up here. I wouldn't have made the summit without you. You must be in the picture with me."

He moved up with surprising spring in his step and took a position on my right, smiling all the way. We each wrapped an arm around the other and waved at the camera. Bill made a couple of exposures and moved back to get a second camera. I suddenly felt very weak and sagged. Once again, Goodluck provided support while Bill completed the pictures.

For one brief moment, Goodluck Christopher and I had been higher than anyone on the entire African Continent. For one brief moment we stood higher than 105 million people. Imagine. I felt a shiver of excitement. Finally the victory registered and everything became warm.

As I sat at the base of the summit rock I was startled by the thought we were also higher than anyone on the Continent of Europe. Mount Elbrus in Russia is the highest peak in Europe and is slightly lower than Kilimanjaro.

We were certainly higher than anyone in the lower 48 states of America.

My mind raced on. We were higher than anyone on the Continent of Australia. Their highest mountain is Kosciusko at 7,316 feet.

We were higher than anyone in Antarctica. Vinson Massif is only 16,864 feet.

In fact the only continents with higher mountains than Africa were Asia, South America and North America (Alaska).

I couldn't resist a final thought. If there were no expeditions at the summit of those three continents, we could very well be the highest human beings in the world. Higher than 4,508,000,000 people.

World Mountains

The highest mountains on the seven continents.

Continent	Mountain	Location	Altitude	
Asia**	Mt. Everest	Nepal	29,028 ft	8848m
South America	Aconcagua	Argentina	22,834 ft.	6960m
North America	Mr. McKinley	Alaska	20,320 ft.	6194m
Africa*	Mt. Kilimanjaro	Tanzania	19,321 ft.	5889m
Europe*	Mt. Elbrus	South Russia	18,465 ft.	5628m
Antarctica	Vinson Massif	Ronne Ice Shelf	16,864 ft.	5140m
Australia	Kosciusko	New South Wales	7,316 ft.	5140m

* Author reached the summit on this mountain.

** Author hiked the Khumbu Valley at 15,000 ft. and sighted this mountain.

Snow was present on most of the rim of the Kilimanjaro crater, except at our position on the southwest edge. When I managed to stand I began taking panoramic photos of the mountain top with a wide angle lens. I went close to the edge of the crater and felt Goodluck's hand on my arm. My wobbling gait did not inspire a great deal of confidence and he saw no need to sacrifice an American climber to gods of the volcano. A good thing.

Even in my exhausted state I was impressed with the size of the crater. It appeared to be about a mile wide and 600 or 700 feet deep at the extreme floor. Looking northeast toward Kenya one could see the massive ice shelves of the glaciers. They appeared to be giant ice steps from inside the crater to the rim and over the side. I counted about eight shelves or steps, each from 20 to 30 feet high. No doubt the glacier steps could inspire fable. Perhaps the gods of the crater would use the steps to climb out of the volcano when they were upset with the world and wished to hurl some lava stones onto the plains just to get the attention of errant human beings. Then again, perhaps my oxygen depleted brain was working too hard.

It became apparent, as I scanned the rim, that we were not on the highest point of the mountain. I was more than a little disappointed. The highest elevation on the crater rim appeared to be directly across from our position.

Goodluck explained to me that Kilimanjaro tradition is that if you reach the crater rim at Gilman's Point (our location) you have reached the top of the mountain. The highest point, just a few hundred feet higher than our position, looked to be a punishing trek over ice and snow and would take several hours. The guides didn't indicate this extra trek was an option. David raised the question and discovered it was possible. Felix did his best to dissuade him. Felix was beat, just like the rest of us and wanted no more of the mountain. David insisted he was going to do it. Felix argued that it was too much. David insisted. And Felix relented. They would go.

To go or not to go was a real non-decision for me. I could barely stand.

To reach the highest point on the rim was a wonderful idea, but as racked as my old brain was, and in spite of a major league headache and growing nausea, reason was not dead. This was as up as I wanted to go. Enough was enough. Anything in excess was definitely too much. Another step up was way too much.

David and Felix prepared to make the final trek. Bruno could not and would not be bested by anyone, so he decided to go. There were no other takers. The rest of us would begin the descent under the watchful eye of Goodluck Christopher, and none too soon. We were all fading fast and needed to get down.

As David and Bruno prepared to go we wished them safe travels. Felix passed close to me and I said, "Pole, pole." He gave me a look of great sadness and simply shook his head. Even the home team was having trouble this high in the heavens.

We began to move to the outer edge of the crater to begin picking our way through the large lava boulders. All began moving in the direction of down except Dwight. He began walking very unsteadily toward the crater. I yelled at him and he kept on going. Perhaps he's going to take one last photo, I thought. Nope, he doesn't have a camera in his hand. Suddenly my heart began to pound in my ears. He is confused.

"Bill, grab Dwight, catch him."

I shouted at Bill since he appeared to be the most mobile. Bill needed no explanation, reacted quickly and soon had Dwight by the arm and was turning him around. He was steps away from a death dive to the floor of the crater. When I saw his face I knew he was in trouble. His eyes were vacant, a real thousand yard stare, the kind you see in shell shocked troops in battle. Dwight was clearly not with us. His skin was pale and he had all he could do to lift his feet. Bill guided him and helped him descend.

I didn't share this observation with the group, but seeing Dwight's serious altitude sickness symptoms I began to fear for David, Bruno and Felix.

It was definitely time to descend. We had been at the top for about twenty minutes.

I returned to the edge of the crater for one last look, raised my camera and made some final photographs. In the corner of the viewfinder I thought I saw a flash. I looked to the right and saw it again. There was a distinct flash of light and it appeared to be coming from the floor of the crater. I searched for the source of the flash. There it was again. Is it a reflection off a piece of equipment, is someone down there? Another flash. Could it be a signal for help? I turned to Bill and was about to say, "Give this a look, something is flashing from the bottom of the crater." But as I looked at Bill I saw a flash, and then another. I looked away from Bill at the vast cloud bank several thousand feet below us and saw another flash. The flashing is in your eyes, Patrick, the flashing is in your brain. It's like that signal on the instrument panel in your car telling you that you are low on fuel or in need of some maintenance. Right on all counts, I thought. I need oxygen. The flashing continued and only subsided as we descended.

At the edge of the crater I looked back at the summit, at Gilman's Point. There was no frozen leopard near the summit.

David, Bruno and Felix were somewhere in the snow field heading for the opposite rim. Goodluck waved me down. What to say? A simple prayer perhaps for the safety of all. At this altitude any prayer is sure to get there faster. I smiled and the smile turned into a lump in my throat. Goodluck waved again and said, "Come, we go down." We had reached the top of Africa. The gods of Kilimanjaro had been tough but fair.

The Descent

As I stepped over the edge to begin the descent I could see a long steep skree field off to the left. The switchback trail we negotiated in the dark hugged the edge of the skree. It was etched into the side of the mountain and reminded me of a delicate necklace on the throat of an old but elegant African lady.

I decided to take one last look from the summit and create a powerful memory. For a moment it seemed as if I were looking at the entire planet, so vast was the view. I smiled at the joy of the moment and thought turned to verse. I located my notepad and a stubby pencil. My writing was shaky and I later had difficulty determining what I had written, but there was nothing shaky about the impression or the lesson I had learned.

> When
> Standing
> At the very
> Top of the great
> Mountain the brain buries
> The pain of persistence and
> The heart sings a beautiful song.

Goodluck directed us to the left, away from the switchback course and over to the skree field. It was loose, not frozen. The skree field went down the mountain for thousands of feet. Walking up a skree field would be a nightmare. It would literally be one step forward two steps back. But going down a loose skree field was another matter entirely. I began to catch on.

Mr. Christopher, knowing a descent is punishing on knees, ankles and hips, which must carry the jolt of total body weight at each step, had decided to test the skree. He liked what he found and motioned us in his direction.

In spite of the psychological lift at the prospect of heading down the mountain toward much more friendly atmosphere I was still very unsteady. My head was pounding and movement, even downward movement, caused gasping for what air there was.

All eyes were on Goodluck as he stepped down the skree field and slid a couple of feet. He stepped down again and slid a few more feet. He was suggesting that we descend in the skree and skate or ski our way down.

No stranger to ice skating or skiing, I stepped off the hard trail and onto the skree with confidence, preparing to assume the skiers bent knee approach and slide a few feet. I landed on the skree, my hiking stick stuck and instead of skiing I pitched forward like a human canon ball. I didn't slide far but my tumble was comic relief for the entire group.

We all began sliding down hill, following Goodluck's example. It was a glissade action used on snow in Nordic skiing and the motion and rhythm came back to me quickly. I would push off on one foot and stride and slide, then push off with the other foot. It was very much like skating downhill. Were it not for the high altitude this would have been a great deal of fun. But any exertion at this altitude is difficult and we were soon stopping and gasping and trying to recover before the next glissade.

At one rest stop I observed that Mawensi was barely visible under the clouds below. It looked so small I was startled. We were very high and Mawensi was a point of reference.

We continued our controlled slide down the mountain for an hour, finally taking a long rest break at Hans Meyer's cave. It is a natural overhang of lava rock at about 17,000 feet. The cave offers some shelter from sun, wind, snow and rain. It served just that purpose on Meyer's ascent in 1889. The Meyer team had spent a cold but somewhat protected night in the cave before resuming the first successful ascent of Kilimanjaro the next morning.

I struggled back to the rear of the cave and nestled down against the wall. The air was better, no question there was more oxygen. The sun emerged with full power and the day was suddenly bright and becoming beautiful. I thought of a John Denver song inspired by the mountains of Colorado. So many of John's songs were inspired by the mountains. I hummed a line: "Sunshine on my shoulder makes me happy." The sun is definitely fuel for the psyche and the soul.

While the group was quiet it was clear that everyone was improving. People were still enjoying private thoughts, but movements were more animated and there was much more physical control. I was particularly happy that Dwight had re-joined us from the never-never land of an oxygen depleted brain. He was smiling, talking and making perfect sense.

I dug into my camera pack, found an orange and enjoyed a banquet. Hunger was returning. A very good sign. I also found that I was now interested in capturing some of the images of the stop. As I was digging a Nikon out of my pack I thought, "Hey, good signs, the guy is eating and wants to take pictures. Recovery is underway."

I aimed a Nikon at the entrance of the cave. Our group was backlit by the sun. As I made the photo it occurred to me that this is the exact image Hans Meyer saw when he awakened almost one hundred years ago in the cave that now bears his name. That thought gave me a shiver.

We saddled up gear and pushed down the mountain, glissading and feeling better by the minute. It was beginning to feel warm and we were only an hour from base camp.

Somewhere on the rim of Kili, David, Bruno and Felix were making their way to the other side of the crater. Snow and ice made the going slow and difficult. They were now just inside the crater rim which protected them from the cold wind. However the intensity of the sun at this altitude made conditions unusually warm, perhaps too warm. The snow became wet and heavy. They began to perspire and removed a layer of clothing. Hydration became an issue for they were carrying only minimal water.

At the outset of their trek the boys set an aggressive pace. After a few hundred feet Bruno actually gave in and told David to continue and he would wait for his return. He did not want to impede progress and ruin David's chance to reach the opposite rim.

"No good, Bruno," said David. "I know how much this means to you. Let's take it slow and we'll make it together. Slow and easy, mate."

David exemplified the true spirit of mountaineering: stick together, help one another, work as a team. David had the kind of integrity and good judgment you want in a partner on a mountain. He was a trusted teammate and with these qualities he proved to be a good leader.

At every stop he reassured Bruno and urged him on. "We'll do it together, mate. We will make it."

The German faltered again. The heat was draining, the sun reflecting off the snow was blinding and the altitude was hammering the three climbers. Bruno, once again offered to stop and wait. David, once again insisted that they would do it together. He helped Bruno along, coaxing, cajoling, motivating . . . while struggling himself. Felix was also having a difficult time.

The Irishman, the German and the Tanzanian made it to the opposite rim, the highest point on the volcano. It was another punishing trek and an extremely satisfying achievement.

None of these men had known each other for more than a few days. Chances were very good they would never meet one another again. Nothing was owed. There was nothing to gain. And there was so much at risk. They could barely speak one another's language, but they communicated in the richest way . . . they helped one another without prompting and they didn't quit.

In the aftermath, Bruno indicated that without David's encouragement he wouldn't have made it.

In a world permeated by the "me first" syndrome, in an "I'm going to get mine" society, in a "horray for me and I hope you fall on your ass" environment where a popular office sign says, "You have probably mistaken me for someone who actually gives a damn" . . . . David's action was a pleasure. It is entirely reassuring to know there are David Shrock's in the world, people committed to values which compel them to take care of someone else. Perhaps it was the coach in him, the teacher. Perhaps it was his own personal connection between head and heart.

Stopping at Hans Meyer's cave was a nice break, however the inactivity began to generate chills. Time to move. Time to let the body work and develop some heat.

We continued glissading down the steep slope, ever closer to the Kibo Hut base camp. At Kibo (15,500 feet) we would change to dry clothing, gather our gear, pack it for the porters and then continue the descent to Horombo Hut (12,300 feet) where we would spend the night. The total descent would be 6,700 feet in one day.

It took less than two hours to descend from the summit to Kibo Hut. It had taken me over seven hours to make the painful night climb to the volcano rim, limping along behind Goodluck Christopher. I was weary, but happy weary, good weary.

As I replayed the events of Saturday and Sunday I realized that we had been awake and moving for over 24 hours with no sleep. When we reached Horomobo Hut later in the day we would have been on our feet going up or down the mountain for 36 hours.

The last real sleep we had was at Horombo on Friday night. We had climbed slowly all day Saturday to base camp where we had spent a cold, sleepless night before beginning our ascent of Kili at midnight. We had climbed through the night reaching the summit at about 7:00 AM. On the descent we would reach Kibo (base camp) at about 10:00 AM and then continue our descent to Horombo arriving there late in the afternoon.

We arrived at base camp, wet from exertion and very much in need of fluid. As we passed the waiting porters they handed us a cup full of cold orange drink. I drained it in one long delicious pull. It was wonderful and I babbled my thanks as I made my way to the shelter. Spirits were high and the porters were smiling at our good fortune. We had all made the summit.

As I packed I began to shake. On the upper slopes, working hard, wet clothes were merely uncomfortable. At base camp the wet clothes became an icy fist. Chills began followed by shaking as muscles vibrated to create some heat. When my teeth began to chatter uncontrollably I knew I was losing body heat at a dangerous rate. I stripped off my clothes as fast as I could, pulled out my duffel, located my sleeping bag and zipped myself in. I was desperately attempting to find some heat and stop the shaking. But the shaking only increased. I brought my knees up to my chest, literally hugging myself. How fragile we are, I thought and how quickly life could end from exposure to moisture and cold air.

While the others continued packing I thought about the contrast between Meyer's 19th Century Kili expedition and our successful climb. Comparatively speaking, our trek had been a walk in the park. We were in good shape, had excellent equipment, guides who knew the mountain and we were all very healthy. In the 19th Century many had died making attempts to ascend Kili. Many had expired more than 6,000 feet below our current position.

Felix appeared and mistook my prone and fetal position as an attempt to sleep.

"No, no, no, no, do not sleep. Up, up. No sleep, please, you must move, move quickly now, up."

Felix knew that going to sleep at this stage could be fatal. As much as I wanted to continue to huddle in the sleeping bag, I knew he was right. Up and moving was the best bet. Many stories are passed around from mountaineer to mountaineer about climbers shaking from the cold, who lie down to rest and never get up again.

I recalled the image of a climber on Aconcagua in Argentina, the highest mountain in South America. He had reached the snow capped summit and completely lost it. He was suffering from extreme hypothermia. He suddenly felt too warm and stripped off his clothing. In his delirium he then decided to sleep. He was found in the snow, stark naked and frozen solid.

Bill packed some of my things since I was shaking so badly I couldn't make my hands work very well. I struggled into a rain suit, shouldered my camera pack and began a wobbly descent to Horombo Hut.

It is hard to say when the shaking stopped, when warmth finally returned. I was conscious of a mild headache but much of the descent to Horombo is a blur. We hiked on throughout the afternoon and reached camp about 5:00 PM.

I sat on the steps of one of the A-frame huts and the events began to sink in. We had made it. No high fives, no shouts of triumph from me, no Mumm champagne celebration, just the deep and very real sense of having set out to do something very difficult . . . and having done it. I was numb but warm and happy. I felt a quiet, calm sort of inner peace. It felt very good indeed.

Thoughts now turned to the fate of David, Bruno and Felix. We gathered in the meadow and took positions which permitted us to look up the mountain for any signs of life.

When you stop moving you begin to feel the effects of the battering your body has been subjected to for over 36 hours. When you stop moving the pain catches up. Technically the brain produces endorphins, natural pain killers. Bless the brain. When you stop the brain begins talking to you and the bitching can become incredible. Feet speak to you of blisters, raw and even bleeding. Knees swell in protest and crack and pop like Rice Krispies when you move or try to get up. The back begins to call for a general strike around the lumbar area. The ego steps aside. Only the heart and lungs continue without protest. At rest they feel they have not had it so good in many hours.

David, Bruno and Felix appeared on the trail above the camp. We shouted and waved. They simply waved back. As they stumble into camp we gave them a loud cheer. I hugged David and tried to lift him off the ground. No luck. Bruno accepted handshakes and much back slapping with genuine humility. Felix simply smiled and shook his head as we applauded his leadership.

It was clear they had suffered from the sun. There were two red faces out of three. Somehow they had found the resolve to make the opposite rim of the crater. It had been a punishing trek. David's unselfish support of Bruno and his commitment to teamwork was, for me, one of the highlights of the Kili experience.

We had put six climbers and three guides on the summit of the highest mountain in Africa and had returned . . . safely.

Day Five On Kilimanjaro
Monday, June 8th

Horombo Hut—The Trek To The Base Of The Mountain

We awoke from the sleep of the dead and were blessed with a crystal clear morning. Bones creaked and muscles protested. Everyone was moving slowly.

In the early morning sun David organized a team picture. It was to be a group photo, six climbers, three guides, seven porters and a cook. Calls in Swahili brought the Africans on the run. I was amazed they could run. Running was the furthest thing from my mind.

Cameras began to appear and, on a jacket on the ground in front of the group, I counted five. We enlisted the help of a Swiss climber who was on the way up. He readily agreed to take the pictures and was impressed that we had all made the summit.

He began with my Nikon and had no luck depressing the shutter. I got up from my position in the front of the group and stepped forward to help him. It was simply a matter of unlocking the shutter release. As I turned to walk back to the group I stopped dead in my tracks. The group picture had become a very big group indeed. Many Africans I had never seen before, were all lined up smiling and posing and enjoying the fun. I laughed and resumed my position in the front row. The more the merrier, I thought. Whatever happened to the native view that cameras steal the soul? The Tanzanians had no reservations. They were grinning ear to ear.

Our trek to the bottom of the mountain would take all day. As we began the long descent, our final day on Kili, I held up the rear in an effort to make some photographs. Felix dutifully remained behind with me, to make sure we were all down the mountain safely. He was determined to be a good steward and be the last one off the mountain. As I would pause to line up a photo, Felix would prop his arms on his walking stick and wait patiently.

I frequently knelt on the ground to examine flowers and plants and to make some close up pictures. It was then I discovered that our quiet Wachagga guide had a sense of humor. Many of the plants resembled the herbs I had seen in the hands of a porter earlier in the trip.

"Are these herbs, Felix? Did the cook use these to flavor our food? Can you eat them?"

"No, sir. Ahhh, then yes, sir. Animals eat plants. You eat animals. You get plants."

We hiked down the mountain for several hours, at first moving slowly and deliberately. As bodies loosened up we progressed to a brisk pace. There was little conversation. Personally I was beginning to think about cold beer at the Kibo Hotel. I could see the condensation on the old cooler behind the bar. The beer now became the carrot on the end of a stick, but I have never confused carrots with hops.

I actually passed several members of our team and found a brisk pace was very comfortable. I passed Bill and he said, "What's the rush?" I simply said, "Beer." And he laughed.

Porters appeared on the trail carrying sacks of gear on their heads and moving up with little apparent effort. When we met them we did the standard greeting.

"Jambo."

"Habari."

"Mizzouri."

It became routine and I did the jambo greeting without even thinking. If the porter got off the "jambo" first, I simply replied "habari" and he was required to say "mizzouri." If I got the jambo off first, then he did the "habari" and I finished the exchange with "mizzouri."

After many such encounters I saw an African coming up the trail without a pack. As he got closer I said, "Jambo."

And he said, "Hey, what's happenin' man, how ya doin?"

I stopped in my tracks and began laughing. And he laughed with me. What a shock. I was conditioned to see a black face, say "jambo" and hear a Swahili reply. He knew this and was having great fun with it.

Howard was from Los Angeles and the first black American mountaineer I had ever met. He knew he was an exception and played his practical joke perfectly. I briefly described our good fortune and gave him what advice I could. We shook hands and then gave each other a brotherly hug and I wished him a successful summit.

As he started up the trail I said, "Howard, just a moment. Let's have some fun. In a few minutes you will meet our team on the descent. There will be a tall, fair skinned, sandy haired guy with glasses. His name is Bill Jackson. He will never in a million years figure you for a climber. I want you to really stick it to him when you pass him on the trail. He will jambo you. Nail him."

Howard began to laugh and his eyes were dancing. He was reading between the lines and promised to do his best. He said Bill's name out loud a few times, laughed and gave me the thumbs up sign. The he disappeared up the trail.

I listened and in a few minutes heard Bill's high pitched roaring laugh. He had seen Howard and given him the African greeting. Howard had replied, "How the hell you doin', Jackson?" And Jackson collapsed. It was a wonderful practical joke.

By mid-afternoon it had become very warm. Everyone shed layers as we got closer to the rain forest. The jungle signaled the beginning of the end of an entire day of downhill hiking. I was in the lead and maintaining a very brisk pace. I had thoughts of beer, food, shower, beer, clean sheets, bed, beer, and sleep. The weather was good and we were about an hour away from the trial head and the Kibo Hotel.

Three porters emerged from the trees some distance below my position. They were moving slowly up the mountain. The last fellow was carrying a ghetto blaster—a combination AM/FM, tape deck with speakers. The music he was playing belonged in an elevator. Now there's a classy ascent, I thought. This must be an interesting team of mountaineers.

And then I sighted the "climbers." He was a bit of a Tom Selleck look-alike; tall, preppy, neatly trimmed mustache, starched and pressed blues jeans, every hair in place. I couldn't believe it. His jeans had a crease and he was spotless. I blinked to try and clear my eyes.

On his arm, walking with easy strides was a very tall and very handsome lady. She wore a twill, tan jump suit with a silk scarf at the neck. Her blonde hair was pulled back, make-up was clearly evident and she was substantially perfumed. The pages of *Vogue*, *"W"* and *Harper's Bazaar* had come to life in the rain forest of Kilimanjaro.

They were both wearing white walking shoes. New white walking shoes.

By contrast I was stained properly with eau du sweat, was five days from the last shower and wore permanently wrinkled clothing that would probably never be clean again.

As they passed, without so much as a "jambo," I looked back. "Tom Selleck" had his arm around her very small waist. A safari hat was hanging off her back. Their hips touched as they walked up the trail. I could smell her perfume at thirty paces. And the music played on.

I searched the trail for Ricardo Montalbon. He was no where in sight. I waited for Herve Villachez to shout, "Da plane, da plane." Nothing.

I blinked, then rubbed my eyes. They were still there, slowly walking up the trail as if it were Rodeo Drive in California, or Worth Avenue in Palm Beach, Florida. What in the heck were they thinking?

Jackson appeared, grinning like the Cheshire Cat. His eyes were absolutely dancing as he did his best Jack Nicholson impression.

"Did you see that? Can you believer that? Technical foul, technical foul! Is that nuts or what? Now I really need a beer."

I had expected the unusual from Africa, but the sight of this couple on a wet and muddy mountain trail, in a rain forest, dressed in starched and pressed, with perfume and music was surreal in every sense.

The Kibo Hotel, once a fading grand dame in the jungle, was now a stunning courtesan. It was a pleasure palace. I dropped my gear and, dirty as I certainly was, headed directly to the bar. The treasure chest of Tanzanian pilsner was sweating and I lost no time liberating a bottle of cool beer. I stood at the bar, wrinkled, sweaty, soiled but triumphant. I had indeed reached the top of Kilimanjaro. Just saying the word gave me a chill. Kil-e-man-jar-oh. Take that Hemingway. I made it. So did your leopard. But the leopard is no longer there. However, the spirit of the leopard is still very much alive. Curiosity and the challenge of climbing a big snow capped mountain at the equator will always capture the spirit of man and beast. And following a climb of Kili it is sometimes hard to tell man and beast apart. I tipped the beer bottle in a friendly direction and just as I did a British gentleman, resplendent in a starched bush jacket (new) and a well crushed bush hat (also new) entered the bar. He looked me over and gave me an expression that indicated I was bordering on untouchable. I may be imagining this but I think he actually wrinkled his nose.

"I take it you have been up the mountain, sir." It was his best imitation of Sir Richard Attenborough, without the empathy.

My appearance indicated I had either been up the mountain for five days or I had very sorry personal hygiene habits. I wanted to say something sophomoric like, "No shit, Sherlock Holmes." I resisted in the name of international relations.

"Yes sir, indeed I have." I extended my hand to make him come closer.

He stepped forward just enough to do a handshake and then withdrew a step.

"Good show, old boy. Did you make the summit?"

I tipped my hat to the side of my head, lifted my beer and said, with the confidence of a James Bond, "Of course."

"Reaaaallllly, old sport. Good show. And what did you find at the top?"

And a voice, which sounded very much like mine, said, "I found two very important things; the end of something and the beginning of something."

He gave a little salute and left as fast as he could.

The climbers gathered with the guides to say our goodbyes. We pooled our money to give the guides and porters a handsome tip. David, who is wise in the ways of the world, suggested a scheme we all quickly agreed upon. Felix deserved the most. He had performed professionally throughout the climb. The assistant guides were to get a little less than the head guide and the rest we would divide among the porters and the cook. David also advised, with Bill very much in support, that we give the money directly to them and not the manger of the Kibo Hotel. We regarded the manager as someone who might sell his mother . . . . twice. While he might still extract a kickback from the guides he would not know how much we had given them. Sad to worry about such things, but we did. No assholes in the mountains? Well, we were at the base of the mountain, so he may have qualified.

In addition to tips it is customary to give the natives a present. They seem grateful for anything you can spare and are not beyond lobbying for items they like: a t-shirt, jacket, or a pair of running shoes.

Our guides and porters lined up in the corridor of the Kibo Hotel. Felix conducted a brief ceremony and presented each of us with a Tanzanian government certificate to prove we had reached the summit of Kilimanjaro.

The Wachaggas filed past us and shook hands. William, the oldest porter clasped both of his hands around mine and gave me a teary smile. He expressed his happiness that I had reached the summit. Evidently Goodluck told him about my struggle. I later learned that he had been to base camp several times but had never gone to the top of the mountain. The income from our expedition would feed his family for some time.

For the Americans the climb was high adventure, a great challenge and a supreme test of will. For the Africans it was substantial income and a way to provide for their families. Both noble pursuits.

At the edge of the crowd I found Goodluck Christopher. Everyone gathered around us for they knew what he had done and what we had been through together. I gave the little giant a hug and everyone cheered. I then took off my glacier glasses. They were REI specials with leather patches on the sides to keep out the glare and they sported a flexible Vaurnet neck cord to keep them in reach at all times. He examined them gingerly, lifted the cord over his head and placed the glasses on his chest.

"Goodluck, I'm grateful for your courage and your patience. I would not have made the summit of this great mountain without you. Thank-you. May the gods of Kilimanjaro bless you and keep you safe. I will never forget you, my friend."

I hugged him again and patted him on the back. Everyone applauded. He placed the very dark glasses on his face. I could not see his eyes, but I didn't miss his smile.

"Safari sana, Mr. Patrick," said Goodluck Christopher. He paused at the door of the hotel, waved his right hand and, with his customary swagger, disappeared into the jungle.

A Night In Arusha

We reclaimed our truck from a fenced in compound near the Kibo Hotel. It appeared to be intact. We feared, with some justification for trucks are treasured in this part of the world, that it might have been carried off piece by piece while we were on the mountain. Not the case.

David, Frankie and Dwight decided to join us for the drive from Marangu to the nearby city of Arusha. Bruno elected to stay one night at the Kibo and then travel to the island of Zanzibar the next day.

As we drove down the mountain road we passed numerous barefoot African children dressed in simple sack-like covers. They were working or playing in the fields and forest. As we passed they would look up and wave or make a hitch-hiking gesture—arm outstretched, palm up, broad smiles.

Their smiles reminded me of my son, Matthew Michael Mages, "M" to the third power. What a contrast. His bedroom was bigger than most native family huts. And he may have had more clothing in his closet than an entire African family. He was into skateboards, computers, drums and rock-n-roll. African kids seemed to be into gathering wood in the forest or herding cattle or goats.

We passed a clearing in the jungle and I recognized the unmistakable shape of a soccer pitch with goal frames at each end. The pitch was built on a slope. The land had been cleared but small stumps remained here and there. Great, I suppose, for learning to dribble well. The goals were nothing more than wooden poles fastened together. There was nothing so luxurious as a net and they didn't have a proper ball. They were playing with a "ball" composed of banana leaves wrapped in natural twine.

As I watched the children I realized how much I missed my son.

The material contrast was a little depressing. They had so little, he seemed to have so much. I scolded myself on this point since the material issues hardly relate to happiness or success. Having or not having material things is all a matter of perception. It is all quite relative.

Were these kids, with what appeared to be little in the way of material things, any happier or less happy than a western child with many material possessions?

They were smiling and finding some pleasure in life. They were animated and very much alive. And they were giving me a great deal of pleasure, because they are children and pretended to be nothing else.

I stuck my head and shoulders out the window and waved both hands and bobbed my head like a clown. They shrieked with laughter, waved back and began running with the truck.

Arusha, we were assured by David The Worldly, meant hot showers, beds, clean sheets and good food. Close, but no cigar.

Bill, Dwight and I stayed at the New Arusha Hotel, which was not new and certainly not much of a hotel. David and Frankie went off to find less expensive digs.

At check-in we encountered the most insolent female desk clerk on the planet. No contest. She was sullen, deaf to male tourists, hostile and, we discovered later, just warming up. While we waited she held a conversation with a friend, ignoring us completely. Then she sat down and read something. We attempted to get her attention. She got up and left. We waited. She returned and struck up a conversation with another friend. I walked over, entered her space and asked politely if we might have some rooms. She gave me a withering expression and with a hand gesture shooed me away.

I don't know if Tanzanians believe in witchcraft, voodoo or the equivalents, but I'm sure she had dolls and long sharp pins under the counter. I'll bet she took great delight in jamming the dull pins into the dolls and in very sensitive places.

It was only after several requests for assistance she finally checked us in without ever making eye contact. No questions were asked, she simply tossed keys onto the desk and walked away.

We found that almost nothing worked at the New Arusha Hotel except the mosquito netting over the beds. That we needed mosquito nets over the beds was somewhat less than comforting.

The world's oldest travel joke must have originated at the New Arusha. First prize, one night at the New Arusha Hotel; second prize, two nights at the New Arusha.

Like Bill, I travel the country helping clients help themselves. In my speeches and seminars I consistently make the point that good service in America is the exception. I now no longer limit my view to America. Good service is a world wide exception. Insolent service personnel exist in every color, every hue, and in every nation.

I taunted Dwight. "Dwight, old boy, I have good news and bad news. The good news is that we have lined up a date for you this evening. The bad news—she is the desk clerk at the New Arusha."

Dwight looked at me with an ever so slight smile, "Hmmmmm, well she is kind of attractive and does have an interesting . . . glare."

After cold baths and a change of dry clothes we met David and Frankie for a late supper. David knew Arusha (no pun intended) and led us to a place called The Chinese Restaurant. I sat across from Frankie. Showered and in skirt and blouse she looked soft and feminine and we were all in love with her.

During the meal, which proved to be very good indeed, David provided entertainment by traveling to and from the alley in back of the restaurant negotiating with a local money changer for a good black market exchange rate. He made at least four trips until his money pouch, which he attached to the front of his belt and hid under a loose shirt, was absolutely bulging.

It turns out that even a good rate of exchange is a bad deal. Tanzanian shillings were not worth much. In fact, one Tanzanian hotel posted signs which clearly stated they would not accept their own money. It apparently is right up there with Parker Brothers Monopoly money in terms of value. They want American dollars and tell you that up front. Once you change bucks into Tan shillings the banks will not change them back to American dollars or any other valued currency.

At one government run hotel, Bill made a point to have me photograph the sign indicating they would not accept their own money. He felt no one in Albuquerque would believe him.

We capped the night with a brandy in the lobby of the hotel. The desk clerk had departed, on her broom no doubt. I did note that Dwight kept looking over his shoulder in the direction of the check-in desk. Brave lad.

From Arusha To The Ngorongoro Crater—A World Wonder

In the morning we explored the shops on the pock marked streets of Arusha. It was a market town, with little or no market. I scanned a news stand for an English language paper. No luck.

We motored out of Arusha on one of Africa's best "A" highways. Dwight had enlisted his own driver and was headed in another direction. David and Frankie also had another destination, although we agreed to meet in Nairobi in two or three days for one last celebration dinner.

Bill and I were off to see the Nogorongoro Crater, one of the most unusual game reserves in the world.

We bounced along the rutted city streets of Arusha among a mixture of native busses, very large overland trucks and two wheeled carts pulled by natives. At the edge of town we waited in line to cross a one lane bridge which spanned a river forty feet below. As we crossed the rickety bridge I looked down and noticed several native women, naked to the waist, scrubbing clothing and children in the muddy brown water.

The Ngorongoro (the "N" is silent) reserve is the floor of an extinct volcano. It has served for untold centuries as a sanctuary for almost every kind of African wild life. We decided it was a must see, in spite of the travel challenge over more rutted and twisting dirt roads.

In route we encountered a road block in the middle of nowhere. Several Tanzanian Army vehicles were parked along the road. Soldiers, looking sullen and bored, were fully armed and simply waiting for bad guys to show up.

We stopped in front of two soldiers holding automatic rifles. They wished to search our truck. We offered no objections.

JOURNEY TO THE TOP OF AFRICA   147

I've been stopped a time or two by American highway patrolmen for driving a mite faster than the posted limit. Imagine that. But, I have never encountered a drawn weapon, except, of course, a long writing ball point pen capable of penetrating two forms on a pad of tickets. Looking into the eyes of an African soldier carrying an AK-47 was damned unsettling.

We were not sure what they were looking for and they refused to communicate. They did a proper job inspecting our gear.

As we awaited our fate I examined our arsenal. It consisted of two Masai hunting spears we had acquired as trophies. In flight, I thought, we would have to be faster than a speeding bullet, or speeding bullets. The soldiers would only have to be faster than a speeding spear. Weighing the odds and the prospect of successful escape took but a second or two . . . maybe less. We would cooperate fully. Of course.

When the soldiers waved us through the roadblock the day became infinitely brighter.

We motored on for several hours in heat, dust, and over ruts big enough to hide a small village. At the entrance to the game reserve we pulled over and joined a queue to pay our fees.

Immediately ahead of us was a large truck outfitted to carry tourists on a platform with benches. It was a camera safari of French tourists and the guide/driver we learned was a moonlighting park official. No doubt he would get special treatment.

We entered the guard shack following the native guide, who knew everyone. He schmoozed and smiled and joked with his colleagues. The fix was in. He put his briefcase on the counter and began to pay the fees for his party of twenty.

Inside the briefcase were several neat stacks of Tan shillings, all similar in size and all held together with rubber bands. I glanced at Bill and we both smiled. It looked like the scene from a crime movie when the gangster displays the payoff loot. I had never seen an entire briefcase full of paper money. Tan shillings are worth so little it took many bundles, a full briefcase, to pay the entrance fees.

We listened as the tour guide explained there was a packet for each person on his truck and the packets were all the same. He hand picked one and gave it to one of the guards to verify. The guard slowly, ever so slowly, counted each and every bill in the packet. Every time his radio/telephone signaled a transmission he would stop, complete the call and then start from the beginning to count again. We groaned out loud at the process.

When one stack was properly counted he reached for another. I thought, "Oh no, he's going to count all twenty packs. We will be here for days." I was relieved when the guide/driver/colleague explained that there was no need to count them all. The guard raised his head, looked at his friend with dull, noncommittal eyes, hesitated as if he were weighing the packet of bills, and began to count again. Bill and I retreated to the corner of the shack.

"He's going to count every last bill. I just don't believe it."

"He doesn't trust his buddy, that's clear. It's near closing time. If we don't make it we may have to stay outside the reserve till morning and there is no place to stay except in lovely downtown Arusha."

We watched. It was like a dream sequence. Everything was in slow motion. Pull off a rubber band, count, pull off another rubber band, count again, phone interruption, start over, pick up another packet, count, etc., etc.

When the guard finally finished it was no surprise to us the count was short. The packets had not been the same. There was a swift and slightly hostile exchange in Swahili. The opponents stared at one another. It was like high noon in a western movie. The face off was occurring. Who would draw their gun first?

The guide finally gave a heavy sigh and drew . . . from his pocket, another stack of Tan shillings and paid the balance, complaining all the way.

We paid our fees, got the rubber stamp treatment and were cleared to proceed to the top of the crater. We motored up the shoulder of the mountain toward a vantage point on the crater rim. It took an hour to negotiate jungle switchbacks and reach the crater viewing area.

Ngorongoro is one of the world's largest volcano craters. The crater on Kilimanjaro had appeared to be about a mile wide. Ngorongoro is many miles wider and now more of a rectangle than a circle, for the sides of the crater have caved in over the centuries. It is approximately ten miles by twelve miles, more than one hundred and twenty square miles of surface and about fifteen hundred to two thousand feet deep in places. I raised my Nikon with a wide angle lens and had to pan and make three exposures to capture the entire scene. The size of the crater was truly amazing.

From our position high above the crater floor we could not see any wildlife. There was a large lake near the center of the crater. It was obviously stagnant and fed by runoff from the crater walls. It had a pinkish haze to it, probably some kind of algae, I thought. I could see large grassy plains and what appeared to be marshy areas near the lake. There was a small forest on one side of the crater floor. Almost every condition was present for almost every type of African wildlife.

Bill went to the truck and I stood on the crater rim making additional photos. I felt a sharp stabbing pain in my right ankle. I slapped at it and moved aside. Then I experienced another sharp pain in the other ankle. And yet another, and another. In desperation I shouted, "What the hell is this?" I jumped away and swatted some more, but the stabbing continued. These are bites, I thought, lots of bites, painful bites and fled to the safety of the truck, stopping to jump and slap and jump again. As I slapped at my legs Bill began his high pitched laugh. It was clearly a dance he had never seen before and one that Arthur Murray doesn't teach. It felt as if fire ants were feasting on the American tourist. In the event Bill failed to notice I shouted at him that the pain was $!!#%&!!# significant. He continued to laugh and I continued to slap and dance all the way to the truck.

The Government of Tanzania operates a lodge on the rim of the Ngorongoro crater. No, they do not take Tan shillings. Yes, they do accept American dollars.

The lodge clings to the edge of the crater rim and glass walls offer a view of the crater floor. We decided to spend two nights in the relative comfort and safety of the lodge. There was a dining room and a bar, which appealed to us. However, the lodge turned the hot water on at 6:00 PM for one brief hour and lights were turned off promptly at 10:00 PM.

In the evening we found the bar, enjoyed what appeared to be scotch whiskey and devoured a meal of roasted antelope. Later we gathered around an open fire with other fellow travelers. Bill, who is not shy and has never met a stranger, entered a conversation with two Americans who were serving with a government agency in Rawanda. They were on holiday and anxious to talk about home.

We learned that African governments are about as stable as the weather, that any statistics about Africa are bound to be erroneous and Africa could be decimated by the AIDS virus.

During the discussion we were joined by Sandra Campbell, a Philadelphia travel agent, on tour alone, exploring tour possibilities in East Africa. Sandra, attractive, fair and blonde, explained that she lived on Rittenhouse Square. It happened I knew a corner bar on the square called "Not Quite Cricket" that featured jazz music. We connected and had a lively conversation about her neighborhood and her travel work.

During our conversation Sandra kept glancing at a very dark Arab gentleman in a suit. He was starring at the blonde American lady. I asked her about his intent and learned that he had been pursing her for a few days and she was not totally comfortable with the attention.

What is it about the American male? It must be in the genes. Lady in distress, genes to the rescue. We instantly decided it was our duty to protect Miss Campbell from the Arab delegation. We also assured her she was in good hands. I pointed out that William was a former University of Nebraska jock and I had graduated from the U.S. Army infantry. I said, with a wry smile, "Sandra, that makes me a trained killer and Bill a professional athlete." We both laughed, but she only smiled, patiently.

I can't recall whether Sandra asked for our help or not, but she was going to get it anyway.

We decided to begin with diplomatic communication rather than a pre-emptive strike. The crater rim is at an altitude of about 6000 feet, thus the African evening was very cool and, while the roaring wood fire provided some warmth, it was still a bit uncomfortable. I took off my navy blue sweater, Sandra quickly accepted it and slipped it on. My PMM monogram over the heart was clearly visible, a rather direct signal to one and all, including the Arab, that Miss Campbell was with us. I was betting he would get the message.

No luck. He continued to stare at the lovely American lady.

Jackson tried body language, and he has a big body. He took a position in front of Sandra, starred at the Arab and gave him the Jackson look that says, "Get lost." It had no effect.

Persistence is the Middle East. Sandra relented and decided to have a few words with him and clear things up. The white hunters watched from a respectable distance while she respectfully declined his company.

When she returned Bill decided to retire for the night and headed to our room. I insisted on walking her through pitch black corridors (power off at ten), feeling my way along the wall to find her door and the safety of her room.

We discovered the door to her room was unlocked. Not a good sign. Holding her arm in the inky black corridor, I guided her down the hall a few steps away from her door. I then cautiously opened her door and slipped into the room, hugging the wall. I waited for my eyes to adjust to the dark. There was enough moonlight coming in through the window to allow me to search the room. No one home. So, I gave Sandra the all-clear message and assured her she was safe.

We agreed to meet the next day and I insisted she lock the door behind me as I left. I heard the lock turn, was satisfied that she was secure and then felt my way along the wall to locate the Jackson-Mages suite.

Bill woke up as I entered and I heard a groggy voice say, "Everything OK?"

I knew he was barely conscious so I counted a few beats and said, in a low conspirators voice, "Sandra's door was unlocked and the Arab was waiting for her, so I really had no choice but to break his knee, take him to the floor and use my Swiss Army knife. Darndest thing Bill, in the dark I couldn't find the right blade. There are so many. I got the can opener by mistake so I just opened him up and finished him off with the leather punch and scissors."

"Unhuh," replied Bill.

"I slide him over the edge of the crater where the lions will no doubt find him and eliminate the evidence. It was all over in a few seconds and I didn't even work up a sweat. But I may need an alibi. Jax, I was with you all night . . . . right?"

"Unhuh. Unhuh . . . . so everything's OK?"

"Yes, William, everything is fine. Sleep well." He had not heard a thing I said.

Ngorongoro Crater, Tanzania
Wednesday, June 10ᵗʰ

Exploring The Ngorongoro Crater—
Truly A Wonder Of The World

Morning, high on the rim of the crater, was misty and cold. Heavy wet clouds hung all along the rim and spilled over the edge a hundred feet or so until they met the warm air rising from the crater floor. The crater was a giant cauldron and it appeared as if a great chef or high priest (one and the same in American culinary circles) was trying to pour a frothy gray mixture into the volcano and the volcano was refusing to accept the offering.

Perhaps the gods of the crater would prefer a vestile virgin. Maybe two. Or a lovely blonde travel agent from Philadelphia. Hard to figure out the preferred sacrifice these days. Gods can be picky.

The floor of the crater was bathed in soft morning sunlight, a marked contrast to the dark clouds surrounding the high rim. Watching the wet clouds dance on the warm air rising from the floor of the crater it became clear to me the crater was a microclimate, a warm greenhouse in a cold mountain range.

We scanned the crater floor for signs of wildlife and saw none.

Bill learned that visitors must obtain a government permit to drive into the crater; yet another permit and another set of African officials with rubber stamps.

After some debate we decided to engage a native guide for this adventure. Driving down into the crater would be a significant challenge and since there were no roads or clear trails in the crater, a guide was an easy decision. The crater is teeming with almost every kind of African wildlife and it is far too dangerous to go on foot, much less alone.

The drive into the crater required a full tank of fuel so we began the day searching for petrol. Motoring through the cloud filled forest on the shoulders of the volcano we passed enormous steaming piles of dung. Elephants had been foraging during the early morning hours. We drove with unusual caution, scanning the brush on either side of the road for large moving gray "rocks."

On the correct assumption that there was but one road in this part of the world and we would eventually arrive at our destination, we motored on. Assumption correct; we had created a good navigational rule for African travel. For good measure we stopped two hiking natives and inquired, proving once and for all that men can and will ask for directions. Following polite assurance that we were on the right track (mind you, the only track) they asked for a lift to the village, which is composed of a petrol pump, a government office for crater permits, and crater guides. We transported them into the village and then decided to split up; Bill to do the petrol duties, Pat to obtain the permit and the guide.

There were three small wooden buildings in the village, open windows, no signs and no doors. I guessed and entered the middle building. It was dimly lit and the counter consisted of a couple of planks supported by posts. As I approached the counter the clerk handed me a permit to fill in and sign. As my eyes began to adjust to the light I realized I was face to face with one of our passengers who smiled broadly and handed me a pencil. We both laughed at this bit of African irony. We had certainly asked the right natives for directions. Laughter is a universal language, particularly when it is at your expense.

Our smiling ex-passenger and government clerk waved his hand and a slight little man with a head too big for his body, emerged from the back room. The clerk introduced me to Godfrey, who would be our guide for the day. Godfrey's eyes were very large, his expression absolutely dead pan and his government issue jacket hung on his body like a rug thrown over a chair.

We collected three box lunches and headed for our truck. Bill had purchased a full tank of fuel. He would drive, I would man the Nikons and make the photographs, while Godfrey would keep us out of trouble and bring us back alive. Alive is good.

Godfrey took up his position in the center of the back seat and said, "Drive, please."

Bill looked over his shoulder with a "Drive where?" expression on his face. He then did a quick deduction and answered his own question, something he does a lot. Conclusion: there was only one direction to go in a one road land—ahead. Bill slipped the clutch on our four-wheel drive machine and off we went.

Godfrey provided just-in-time directions and soon we were poised on the edge of the crater rim with the nose of the truck pointing at the crater. Godfrey said, "Drive on." And Bill carefully and slowly drove ahead. At one point all we could see through the windshield was sky. A few breathtaking feet later the truck nosed over the rim and we were suddenly starring down at a very steep and rocky switchback more suited to hikers than truckers. The adventure was on. I made a mental note to thank Bill for driving, should we make it back.

The truck, very reliable up to this point, behaved poorly. It sputtered and died, re-started and sputtered again as we descended fifteen hundred feet or so down into the crater. We chalked this up to the angle of descent, the rocking, bumping and general torture the truck was receiving.

We passed Thompson gazelle, a lion lazing on the plain, an ostrich and birds we had never seen before. The crater had come to life. Animals and birds we could not see from the distant rim were now all around us. It was like being in a zoo without walls. Or ceilings. I turned to Bill and said one word, "Incredible."

Centuries, many centuries ago, when the volcano had blown its top and cooled, the sides began to erode and the crater eventually filled in. Animals found their way into the crater and countless generations later they live out their lives breeding, hunting, being hunted, eating or serving as the supply end of the African food chain—seldom, if ever, leaving the floor of the long extinct volcano crater.

Ngorongoro Crater is a patchwork quilt of African vegetation, animal and bird life. It is a sampler of an entire continent. In this one hundred and twenty square mile refuge we encountered dry plains, dark forest, a large shallow lake, plenty of marshland and grassy meadows—every habitat necessary to support the animal kingdom of Africa. It is a natural sanctuary and one of the most remarkable places on the planet.

Driving into the crater is very much like visiting an extraordinary zoo, but seeing it from the inside, shoulder to shoulder with bird and beast. It is one of the few places in Africa where one can see what is known as "the big five"—lion, leopard, buffalo, rhino and elephant.

Our truck was like a small metal and glass life preserving capsule which, once inserted into the crater, permitted us to circulate through this very special world and out again, leaving the crater very much the way we found it and creating memories that would last a lifetime.

I asked Bill to pull to a stop so I could photograph a lone lioness engaged in a starring contest with a single large black bird. Twenty feet was all that separated them. I clamped zoom lens on my camera and waited for the lion to spring. It was an exciting scene—the predator eyeing a breakfast snack, the bird fair game. Which would move first?

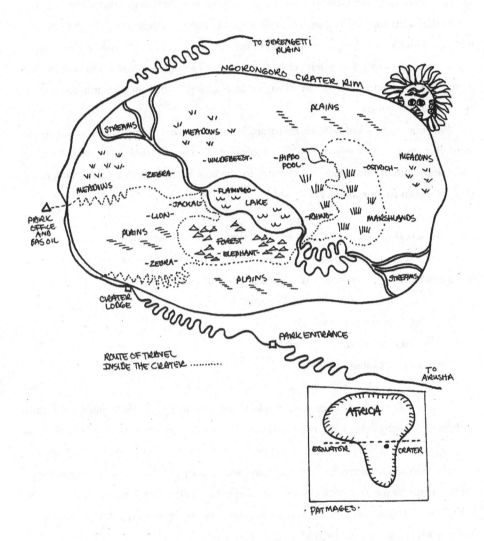

**Ngorongoro Crater Game Reserve
And Route Of Travel Within The Crater**

Most mountain adventures at this point in my life had been solo trips. The luxury of traveling alone is being able to give in to impulse and intuition, to seize a moment or simply spend as much time as it takes to make wonderful photographic images, images that will last longer than a lifetime. When traveling with someone else it is frequently difficult to explain why you wish to wait a long time for just the right moment in which to make a photograph. However, if you love photography, chasing an image or a potential image, watching life and seeing life in greater detail than most, or attempting to put imagination on film or chip . . . requires patience.

Bill became impatient, which is his nature. He's a go-go kind of guy, so he cranked up our sputtering truck and we were off. I don't know if the lion got the bird. Just as well. Death is the ultimate pain in the ass and I was cheering for the bird. I later learned that lions rarely chase birds, not even for hors doeuvers.

The next stop on Godfrey's silent itinerary was the shore of a shallow lake called Lake Magadi. Like many places in Africa it has a second name. It is also called Lake Makat. The second name idea helps keep foreigners off balance and it really works.

"Can you tell me the way to Lake Magadi?"

"No, but I know the way to Lake Makat."

"Well, I'm really intent on finding Magadi."

"So sorry, sir, cannot help you."

From the rim of the volcano crater the lake shimmers in reflected light and has a distinct pink haze. Viewing it from the rim I speculated the color was from some type of algae or mineral. Up close, from the shoreline, the pink haze becomes a glorious sea of flamingos.

I had never seen as much of anything, alive and in one place. Never. It was impossible to tell how many flamingos were feeding or drinking in the shallow lake. One hundred thousand or more would be my guess. Some were making low level flights along the surface, some were sleeping while standing on one leg.

As I raised my camera, Bill became very excited at the scene. "Pat, Pat shoot the one standing on one leg, get a shot of the one standing on one leg." I panned the scene looking through my view finder. "William, any particular flamingo? There are only a few thousand standing on one leg. Is there a particular flamingo?" The only reply I got was Bill's high pitched laugh. He was like a kid at Christmas. The scene did make one giddy.

As I photographed the "pink haze" through an open window (Godfrey insisted we stay in the truck at all times) an animal resembling an underfed coyote padded across the sand about thirty feet from the truck. One word from Godfrey got our full attention, "Jackal." I made one fast image of the jackal, conscious of the open window of the truck and the location of the window crank. Jackal. A small deadly package one could easily underestimate.

The jackal probed the shoreline, scattering flamingos as he went, testing their powers of observation and watching for a potential lunch.

"Drive, please," said Godfrey.

Bill stopped the truck at the edge of a stream which fed the lake. It was a muddy, slow moving tributary and it was clear we would have to cross. Bill turned to Godfrey, whose perpetually passive expression gave us unrealistic confidence. "Drive, go slow."

Bill selected first gear, checked the four wheel drive lever (it was in gear) and we slowly moved forward off the bank and into the stream. It was impossible to see the stream bed for all the silt, however there were tracks emerging from the other side and they gave us a firm line of sight and direction for the crossing. It had been done before. More comfort.

Bill move forward, all four wheels now into the stream. We inched along. Water quickly rose to the bottom of the doors as we settled onto the bed of the stream. The sensation was more boat than truck. Suddenly the wheels were not biting into anything very solid and our progress went from meager to none. Water was rising above the wheels.

"Keep it moving, William, don't stall, don't stall." I reasoned that as long as the engine was running and forcing exhaust out the tail pipe we were all right. As long as the engine was running we could rock ourselves out.

The engine died. The silence was deafening.

All eyes jumped to Bill and the ignition switch. Seconds passed. And then a day. And then a week. Brown water swirled past the stationary truck.

Bill twisted the ignition key to engage the starter and stood on the clutch as if it were a snake attempting to go up his pant leg. He gripped the steering wheel for leverage and his knuckles became bone white. The starter engaged and the engine came to life. EKG waves spiked and jumped off the scope. He gunned the engine and it roared as he shifted into reverse. The wheels spun, suddenly caught solid stream bed and we rocketed backward, harshly but decisively, while visions of Polaris missiles danced in my bobbing head. Water flew everywhere and then mud and sand. Bill actually had to jam on the brakes to bring us to a stop.

We now had real time experience with the expression "when the dust settles." It did and we were starring at the opposite bank, but we were high and dry and breathing deeply. Godfrey seemed bored.

Still clutching the steering wheel, leaving his finger prints forever on the truck, Bill rested his forehead on his hands.

"No more water, Godfrey . . . . no more water."

Later we would laugh about the aborted stream crossing, the dead engine, the cost of the truck and the picked over carcasses of two white adventurers and an African guide. I somehow wondered whether Godfrey would have received favored treatment. After all, he was a local. At least, I surmised, the animals would have eaten him last . . . perhaps used him as a toothpick.

Bill noted that our truck was equipped with a winch on the front and a steel cable.

"Hell, Pat we could have pulled ourselves out, no sweat."

"Ah, yes, but William, the nearest tree is a mile away."

"Hmmmm. True."

"No more water."

"Not even in the scotch."

We reached the edge of a great marsh and pulled through deep, fender high grass. Godfrey indicated we would stop here for lunch. Here was on the bank of large deep pond. The pond was home to a dozen hippos, munching vegetation and displaying molars the size of fence posts. We rolled down the windows and watched the show.

Occasionally a hippo would roll over, doing a 360 in the water with the agility of a sea lion. Watching an animal as big as a building roll over in the water was one of the most incongruous visions of my short life.

We had obtained simple box lunches. Bill and I examined the contents and quickly passed both boxes to the backseat. Godfrey seemed delighted and we saw a hint, just a glimmer of expression. He finished everything but the cardboard. We dreamed about food we could understand. I was tempted to ask Godfrey if he was related to an Irishman named Shrock.

I concentrated on one particularly large hippo. Large hippo may be a classic redundancy, but there were a few much bigger than the others. This one seemed to be the class of the pond. Every now and then it would blow air thru its nostrils causing water to mist in great proportion. Imagine a nostril the diameter of a gallon paint can.

Something moved just to the right of the large hippo. I zoomed in and through the view finder, discovered the large hippo was a mom and she was shielding a baby hippo, keeping it against the opposite shore. The little fellow, about the size of a Volkswagen Beetle, did his or her best to get away, but mom prevailed, no doubt conscious of the intruders with a camera.

From the hippo pool we began backtracking. The driving was a nerve wracking test and Bill was doing a wonderful job.

Bill followed Godfrey's minimalist directions. We skimmed through meadows and plowed and skidded through marshlands. Often the view was grass taller than the hood of the truck. Grass, grass, grass and nothing more except blue sky. For a driver it is the ultimate dilemma; vision was lousy and conventional wisdom would say "go slow." But the marshlands beneath our wheels and our survival instincts, commanded that Bill keep the truck moving and moving fast.

From time to time the ever passive Godfrey would say, "Drive on, drive on." Bill and I kept bracing for the gully or ravine that was sure to appear suddenly through flattened grass and propel us through the roof or windshield. I tightened my seat belt until it nearly arrested my circulation. Later in the day I found impressions of the belt line across my stomach.

Every now and then we would experience a terrific jolt. Always verbal (brevity is not in our lexicon) Bill and I would occasionally shout or curse. The language was sometimes only garden variety, "Oh, shit!" From time to time we would get really creative, but "Oh, shit" became the favored expression of choice. We found that it also translated directly into Swahili, for every time Godfrey heard, "Oh, shit" he would grab for a handhold. But he always remained in character and never changed expression.

We motored on to a destination known only to our stoic guide. Worse than the jolts and uncertainty, which caused us to drip inside our clothing, was the sound of water under our wheels and a momentary loss of power followed instantly by a surge of RPM's. The tires would spin until they found a purchase and we would leap forward again. Tense and sweating profusely, we could see no track, only a sea of grass. Godfrey would wave us on with a flick of the wrist which said, "It is nothing, drive on."

"Here, here, go slow," said the guide. "Rhino, maybe."

That got our attention. Rhino is one of the deadliest animals in Africa.

Bill braked and we began scanning the grass for the big prize in the camera safari world—the fabled black rhino. Our wily expressionless veteran of countless trips to the crater floor did not let us down. Bill motored ahead very slowly until Godfrey signaled with his hand and then pointed to our right. We were flank to flank with one of the most dangerous animals in the world.

Black rhinos are highly endangered. In 1965 the crater rhino population was about 100. By the mid 1980's poachers killed all but a two or three. The government stepped in and organized a 24 hour watch by armed rangers. Because of the rhino's long gestation their numbers have increased very slowly. There are now seventeen.

The rhino was in perfect profile to us, as we were to him. The pre-historic looking animal was feeding. Its silver gray hide was encrusted with mottled patches of mud and scaling skin. An ever present companion, a hitchhiking bird, was busy pecking insects and dead skin from its back. Two tusks, one long and one short, curved toward the sky. It could, no doubt, open the thin metal skin of our truck like a can opener going through aluminum foil. Happy thought. We watched. In awe. No words to say.

The Ngorongoro Crater is one of the last places you can still see wild black rhino. There are reported to be twelve somewhere on the Serengeti Plain, but they are apparently very difficult to find.

The rhino is rock solid, extremely fast and with head lowered and horns fixed on target, a formidable beast. To create some balance in what would be a decidedly unbalanced fight, the rhino was given poor eyesight. Apparently this did not create a great deal of parity for I leaned that many of the early explorers of the crater were killed or maimed by earlier relatives of the animal just forty yards from our truck. I noted that Bill kept one had on the shift and one on the steering wheel as we watched for any sudden movement, particularly movement in our direction.

The rhino fed. He had no interest in Spam-in-a-can. I photographed as quietly as I could but the shutter sounded like a canon. The rhino continued to ignore us while we continued to watch its every move.

We spoke in whispers that would have pleased Bud Collins at Wimbledon. Then slowly, ever so slowly, the rhino turned his head in our direction and we were looking straight at the point of two horns. It was the first time in my life I had actually been confronted head on by the horns of a dilemma.

Without any communication from Godfrey, Bill slowly motored on.

We drove toward a small strip of forest hoping to find lion or elephant. No luck. Godfrey then directed us up the gentle slope of the crater floor to another rocky switchback trail which would take us up about 1800 punishing feet to the crater rim. The truck sputtered and protested all the way.

While in the crater we had seen Thompson gazelle, wildebeest, zebra, hippo, lion rhino, elephant, buffalo, jackal, hyena, ostrich, countless birds even Godfrey could not identify . . . and every flamingo on the African continent (or so it seemed).

We did not see any primates (baboons or monkeys), although there are many in the crater. Nor did we see giraffe. Apparently the giraffe have left the crater simply because there are not enough acacia trees to feed them.

Some of the images of the trip still remain—black and tan zebra against the soft golden grass of the plains, the gray-green walls of the crater, the subtle pink undulating wave of tens of thousands of flamingos, and the rhino, silver gray against the green grassland.

We dropped Godfrey at the park barracks. I helped him out of the backseat and offered my hand in thanks for his guidance. His hand was small, soft and lighter than a child's. He squeezed my hand gently and his mask finally slipped. He actually smiled.

At the crater lodge we sat in the late afternoon sun, looked down into the crater and re-lived our day and re-traced our path. The Ngorongoro Crater is a world heritage site and is referred to as the 8th wonder of the world. I tried to imagine the size of the original volcano as it once towered over the Serengetti Plain. The volcano cone we view today is obviously much smaller in height than the original mountain, thanks to many centuries of erosion. As a volcano explodes it sends incomprehensible quantities of lava rock and ash thirty to forty thousand feet into the sky where it is whipped around the world by jet streams. In time, the cone formed by the blast erodes. The mountain is then reduced in size again with the next eruption. Each explosion reduces the size of the volcano.

As I thought about this progression I felt a little chill. Just how high was the original mountain? The crater is now ten by twelve miles. I drew imaginary lines into the sky from each side of the crater rim and when they met I attempted to estimate the probably size of the mountain. The mountain must have been at least as high as Kilimanjaro. Debris from the monster must have been scattered around the world many times. Somewhere in Texas or Nebraska there might be a piece of the African plain.

We spent our final evening at the Crater Lodge huddling around an open wood fire, consuming large bottles of Tanzanian beer and once again re-living our day in the crater. It was, we agreed, one of the great adventures of a lifetime.

At dinner we again had the pleasure of Sandra Campbell's company. She had also obtained a guide and had been driven into the crater. She echoed our enthusiasm for the experience and described her day. Her eyes teared a little as she attempted to explain the wonder of her experience and we both agreed that words were really inadequate. It is easy to run out of adjectives when describing the thrills of Nogorongoro. Bill and I listened with unusual dedication to her every word. Male bonding, I concluded, had its limits. We were in the company of a very attractive and interesting lady. I said little. Bill did not even interrupt.

Mid-way through plates of antelope a native waiter appeared at our table with a bottle of wine. It was, he said, from a man at the bar who wished to pay his respects to Miss Campbell. I turned, out of curiosity, and exchanged eye contact with the man at the bar. It was the man we had mistakenly identified as an Arab. Sandra got up and spoke with him, discovered that he was not an Arab, but a Sikh. The wine was served, we raised our glasses to him, and sipped.

This was our first experience with African wine. Bill and I have pretty good palates, however Bill is much more knowledgeable about wine and has tasted his way through many countries. I have limited experience with fine wines, but a good deal of experience with abundant good wines. Abundance is a fine quality.

The wine was a Tanzanian product called Dodoma, from the village of the same name. To be charitable, the name captures the quality of the wine. We pronounced it Do-dull-ma.

Dodoma, we decided, reminded us of a wine brewed in Texas. It's called Llano. Bill, who favors very select award winning California and Australian reds, quickly agreed that Llano was unimpressive wine. Being slightly inebriated (pleasantly so) and into our Peck's bad boy routine, we decided that Llano (pronounced Lon-oh) rhymed most assuredly with guano. It was a crude comment, to be sure, and not a true representation of wine made by the good folks at Llano. Sandra, much more a lady than we were gentlemen, described us as, "very bad boys." But she was smiling.

Reaching into his vast storehouse of important and eclectic knowledge, Bill then pointed out that llano is actually the Spanish word for "plain." How perfectly appropriate.

We said our reluctant good-byes to Sandra and learned that she would be touring the Masai Mara game reserve the next day and would then return to Nairobi on Friday. We noted the coincidence (we would also be in Nairobi on Friday) and suggested getting together for dinner, since we would all be in the same neighborhood. We were beginning to sound like real jet set material. "I say, old girl, let's meet in Nairobi for dinner. What?"

I, once gain escorted Sandra down jet black corridors to her room and this time did not have to sweep her room for intruders or dispatch anyone with my Swiss Army knife.

Ngorongoro Crater, Tanzania
Thursday, June 11ᵗʰ

Arusha, Namanga, Nairobi

As we bucked and cursed our way down the rutted track to Arusha, in route to the dreaded border crossing in Namanga and on to Nairobi, we replayed our last evening at the Crater Lodge. We had met an American trade official (Charlie) and his associate (Ted) from the State Department office in Rawanda. Bill and I were curious about their work and their views of Africa. Bill led with questions.

"So, Charlie, how about the AIDS problem? We've heard there are several hundred thousand cases in Africa?

"It is difficult to know. Africans keep very poor statistics when they keep them at all. There could be twice that many, who would really know? You cannot trust African numbers."

"Why Rawanda, why live outside the States?"

Charlie cited the adventure and the educational value of the experience. The posting would also help his career path in civil service. He also mentioned the satisfaction of making matches between African governments and American commerce. He made it clear that Africa could be very difficult and even shocking to the uninitiated.

"Recently we had a young replacement arrive at our mission. He is a young, black, Harvard educated American and has committed to two years of African service. After a few weeks I took him to lunch and inquired about his reaction to Africa. During our conversation he startled me with the following exchange."

"Thank God for slavery," he said.

"What? Why do you feel that way?"

"Well, if it hadn't been for slavery, I would have been born and raised here."

Bill then brought Ted into the conversation. He had the non-committal air of the bureaucrat and his expression and his tone of voice suggested that he knew something, but he wasn't about to tell you.

"So, Ted, where have you served?"

"Here and many other countries."

"Like, where before Africa?"

"South America mostly."

"Countries?"

A long pause. He was trying to decide whether or not to answer.

"Argentina."

"No kidding," responded Jackson, who would now go for the throat. "Were you there during the Falklands War?"

Long pause.

"Yes."

Mega-byte Bill processed this in a nanosecond.

"Wow! Argentina had to be great duty. Why Rawanda?"

"Yes, Argentina was great duty."

He side stepped the Rawanda question. But Bill wouldn't let him get away.

"So, Ted what was your work in Argentina? Classified stuff?"

A long pause.

"No, I was in public information."

He tried to lead Bill astray, but Bill was the mongoose after the snake.

"Really? Were you there at the start of the Falkland conflict?"

Long pause. Ted knew that Charlie knew and a fib here wouldn't help him.

"Yes."

"Did you know it was going to happen before it happened?"

A look of surprise and then chagrin passed across Ted's face.

"No."

And that was how Ted wound up in Rawanda. First prize, one year in Rawanda, second prize, two years in Rawanda. You are probably a spook masquerading as a PR guy in Argentina. Your job is to know things, important things. Like, when a government is going to attempt to heist some land from our most trusted ally and the President's close friend, Mrs. Thatcher.

And you blow it. And you get sent directly to Rawanda, you do not pass "GO" and you do not collect $200.

Our truck coughed every time I downshifted. Huge black clouds of exhaust would appear. The black clouds were ominous. The truck was sick and becoming sicker by the mile

New fears entered the road to Nairobi scenario. Our most pressing question had been whether or not we would make it past the guards at the border. The number one question at this point—will our truck make it to the border crossing? Question two—when will the engine blow or quit?

The condition of the road made it impossible to travel fast. I was driving in second gear much of the time. When I did manage to shift into third gear my hopes would soar for the exhaust would lighten up. Then with every down shift the black exhaust reappeared and hopes were dashed once again. There was no AAA road side service, there were no road side service stations, no help at all and we had a Kenyan truck in a foreign land. A bad deal.

I was actually glad to see Arusha and give the truck a rest. We limped into town, coaxing the truck along. It was sputtering and threatening to die and the black exhaust was becoming worse.

We decided to stop and refuel the truck. We also agreed to take a walk and spend the rest of our Tan shillings. It was hard to believe that the banks would not change our Tanzanian currency back into U.S. dollars. If we returned to the States with Tan shillings the exchange rate, we decided, would be a very bad rate, therefore the best option was to buy what we could.

Bill went after batik while I purchased some dark green malenchite crosses fashioned by the local nuns from the same order that had named and raised Goodluck Christopher. The design of the crosses was medieval and the stone, native to Tanzania, was a beautiful warm green.

Leaving Arusha we enjoyed the luxury of a paved road. I cranked up the sick truck and headed north for Namanga and the border crossing from hell. We made a lot of black exhaust in first and second grear. With third and fourth gear the color of the exhaust seemed to improve. But engines don't heal on their own, so I remained tense, listening for any hint that the engine was about to protest vigorously.

We explored alternatives to the border crossing at Namanga. Our first experience, Kenya to Tanzania, had been so disturbing we actually considered leaving the highway and going cross-country. Our options, we realized, were few and we soon decided to put some steel in our backbones and show the border guards some attitude.

As we approached Namanga I noted with some disbelief that the truck appeared to be healing. The clouds of black exhaust were almost gone, even in first gear.

We had driven some of the worst tracks across the Great Rift Valley and had motored across the lower Serengetti to Nogorongoro Crater. The truck had taken a beating. As we negotiated the crater, driving down rocky switchbacks, splashing through meadows and marshes, back up the switchbacks and on to Arusha we had trailed clouds of black exhaust. We both thought the truck was dying. And now it seemed to be coming back to life. Truly amazing.

Namanga appeared like a bad dream. I pulled up to the Tanzanian customs building. It was chaos. The air was hot and a massive crowd was churning in front of the long counters. The room smelled of sweat and excrement, with an occasional blast of noxious perfume. The crowd pushed and shoved and vied for the attention of a few guards.

The African border guards were irritated and treating everyone with indifference or anger. I decided I would take no abuse from the African officials.

When my turn came, I presented my passport and truck papers and to my surprise received a stamp, stamp, stamp without any eye contact from the guard. That's it. Less than five seconds of official Africa and we were released and cleared to cross. One down and one to go.

We crossed to the Kenyan side of the border. As I left the truck a military guard stopped me, unslung his rifle and asked for my destination. I explained, with as much confidence as I could muster, that our intent was to clear customs and return (I stressed the word "return") to Kenya. He looked at my passport and truck papers and quickly handed them back.

"OK, you go. You go to Tanzania, you come back. Kenyan truck. It's good. You go now." He pointed down the road. Much too good to be true.

I thanked him more politely than his action deserved and walked back to the truck as fast as I could without appearing to flee.

"What's up big guy," said the Bill, with the worried expression.

"I can't believe it, we are free to go."

"Then let's go before they change their mind. Now!"

I gunned the truck (no black smoke) and headed for Nairobi, barely able to contain a shout of victory and relief.

"Wait a minute. Stop. Stop the truck." Jackson was thinking again. "Don't we need to have our passports stamped? They stamped us out of the country, but not in. When we leave Nairobi they will wonder how we got back into the country. They could detain us."

"Damn," from the driver, "damn, damn, damn."

With an almost overwhelming reluctance I turned the truck around and headed back to the Kenyan officials and their rubber stamps.

I could still see the smug face of the guard who derided our efforts to take a Kenyan truck into Tanzania the week before. "What makes you think you can take that truck out of our country? Who gave you the right? You cannot, I won't allow it."

He was, of course, looking for a pay off. None came and he didn't like it one bit. I then recalled the incongruity of his parting shot when we threatened to go back to Nairobi and report him. "We try," he said with a grimace masquerading as a smile, "to be nice to tourists."

As precious as life most certainly is, I wanted to strangle him with my bare hands, slowly and with malice.

I joined a long line of natives in another hot and crowded room. I watched and listened as the guards dished out invective and abuse. One particularly nasty scene played out between a guard and a very slight young woman in robes traveling with two small children. Whatever answers she was giving him in a soft, respectful tone he hammered back with anger and just inches from her face. She was afraid and her children were cowering and clinging to her robes.

After a few minutes of this disgusting behavior I allowed myself the pleasure of boiling over. I took a deep breath, faced the guard with hands on my hips, fists clenched and shouted at him. "Hey! That's enough, dammit. Treat this lady with some respect. What the hell is wrong with you?"

His head jerked up and he glared in my direction. Her eyes were suddenly very large and her children put their faces in her robes and attempted to hide as best they could.

"What business is this of yours?" spat the guard. His words were tough, but his expression told me he was a bit nervous. The classic bully being called out.

I stepped toward him and got as close as the counter allowed. "When you frighten women and children it's everyone's business. I want to see your boss. Who is in charge here? Get him, now!"

He stepped back. I had hit the one nerve that African border guards understand. They all report to someone and fear for the loss of a cushy job.

He glared at me for a second or two, handed the lady her papers and left the room. She vanished without a word. I was boiling mad. I had vented pent up anger and it felt very good.

Although I wasn't sure how this would end, I was prepared to be aggressive and demand better treatment.

Wait, wait, wait. No reappearance of the bully.

As I waited for the guard, Walter Mitty appeared in the form of the late Milwaukee novelist John D. MacDonald. I had read every John MacDonald novel. He created a modern day roving knight, a hero called Travis McGee. Travis, obviously MacDonald's alter ego, is an ex-athlete, ex-soldier, beach bum living on a houseboat at Bahia-Mar in Fort Lauderdale. He won the boat, which he named "The Busted Flush," in a poker game. Travis is built like an NFL tight end, drinks good British gin on the rocks and calls himself a "salvage consultant." He finds things for worthy people and applies force as needed to achieve justice. MacDonald's description of McGee in a fight is to a novel as a good pathologist is to an autopsy report—very detailed and clinically accurate.

I imagined how MacDonald might describe a fight between the American mountaineer and the bullying border guard.

I smiled at the guard as he came at me with a raised fist. I stepped inside the swing and kneed him in the groin. His head snapped forward at the stomach-turning pain, his eyes wide open in disbelief. I assisted him with my right hand, applying firm pressure and forcing his head down. As his head was propelled downward with considerable force, I brought my left knee up and met his face. His nose was the first to go. It crumbled to the side with a crunching as cartilage separated and flesh tore. His nose was forced against his right cheek with such pressure that it made a visceral squishing sound as the cheek bone gave and fluid and blood began leaving his nose. His head snapped back from the collision with my knee. As he jerked into a standing position I grabbed his shirt at the shoulders with both hands, grabbing as much cloth as I could and twisting my hands to get a firm grip. I placed my left knee in his stomach, avoiding my right knee, which was weak from an old soccer injury, and rolled, back first, onto the ground pulling him down with me and then pushing him up with my feet and over my head, propelling him into the thick, rough stone wall of the guard house. There was a thumping sound, much like a gunny sack full of ripe cantaloupes hitting an immovable object. I leaped up, spun around, dropped a knee onto his heaving chest and finished him off by chopping both sides of his neck along the carotid arteries with the edge of both of my hands, in one swift and fluid motion.

He would never again hassle another traveler at the Namanga border crossing. No more harsh words of intimidation from this border guard.

As I left, I tossed off an Ian Fleming/James Bond farewell. "Now then, don't become too choked up at my departure, my good man."

I thought of another. *"You could have saved face, old boy, by just being a bit more civil."*

And another. *"Don't bother getting up old skate, I'll see myself out. May I use your rubber stamp? Right, thanks."*

Following this fictional scene, which took less than ten seconds, the guard recovered fully, without so much as a scratch and resumed his duties . . . . but with new found courtesy and diplomacy. No one actually dies or gets maimed in my day-dreams. Behavior modification, yes. But no deaths.

The guard I had just dispatched, in precise MacDonald fashion along with Ian Fleming bon mots, returned and quickly took my passport, stamped it without hesitation and slid it back to me without a glance. I thanked him and left.

The power of dreams.

The drive from Namanga to Nairobi was uneventful save for one touching event. I had to brake for a herd of giraffes and finally came to a complete stop in the middle of the road. The giraffes decided to congregate on the road and nibble on leaves high in the trees. I actually set the brake on the truck, shifted into neutral and got out to get a full view of the three story animals.

Something small and dark darted onto the road. A native boy, perhaps eight or nine years old, was not pleased with the giraffes so he darted between their legs and under their bellies, swinging a long wooden spear. He actually left his feet as he swung at the hind quarters of the majestic animals. The animals were so tall that their rear ends were at least five feet above the boy's head. He was fearless.

After several well placed whacks the lead giraffe lurched ahead setting an example for the rest and the road cleared quickly, the smiling little boy in pursuit, swinging his spear.

The sight of this tiny, skinny African child dodging giraffe legs and moving tons of lumbering animals with nothing more than a carved stick, made me more than a little ashamed of my fear of the border guards.

Up to this point I had stopped on Wisconsin highways for stray guernesy cows, on Irish lanes for sheep and on French streets for French. Now giraffes were added to the list. Ah, the wonder of travel.

We entered Nairobi, which had improved greatly since we left, and returned to the Norfolk Hotel. Frankie and David had left a message and offered to spend Friday with us. We were very pleased with the prospects of a final day in Africa, led by the indefatigable David Shrock.

Giraffes blocked the road.
A very small boy with a very
large spear took exception.
He darted among their legs
and had to jump in the air
to reach their flanks.
The giraffes had the
good sense to move.

It seemed like a year between visits to the Norfolk. We had been on the plains, in the wilds, up the mountain, down the mountain, up rutted switchbacks, in and out of a volcano crater and moving constantly for something more than a week and a half. We enjoyed an endless supply of hot water, around-the-clock electricity and the latest news, courtesy of the BBC.

I showered once and the tub became dark with dirt. I cleaned the tub and showered again. More dirt. Finally I soaped my entire body, rubbed the soap into my skin vigorously, repeated the entire process with shampoo and then stood under the jets until the water ran clean. The dirt had literally come off in layers.

Perhaps the most interesting experience of all was looking into a mirror for the first time in ten days and seeing a somewhat familiar face. Somewhat in the sense that I now sported a stubble almost long enough to be called a beard. I had purposely given up shaving and was surprised to find the whiskers were coming in red and, black and gray. I resisted the temptation to shave and decided I would take the beard home and enjoy a few laughs and some good-natured kidding.

Once clean, we headed directly for the Lord Dellamere pub at the entrance to the hotel. The pub is an open-air meeting place and semi-famous for having been blown up in a student uprising a few years earlier.

We enjoyed a few bottles of Tusker, the local beer, and were once again surprised at how much the beer had improved since we departed Nairobi for Kilimanjaro. A local told us that the charging bull elephant on the Tusker label and the very name, Tusker, were the result of a tragedy. Evidently, the two English brothers who founded the brewery were enjoying the plains when they were attacked by a bull elephant. One of the brothers was killed. The surviving brother chose the name and created the elephant label. Cheers.

Fortified with a few beers we worked with the hotel switchboard operator and managed to link to the States. I called home and reported to son Matthew and wife Carol that the "eagle had landed"—we were safely up and down the mountain. It was their first experience with a trans-oceanic, inter-continental phone call and they were surprised at the clarity of the connection. Hearing familiar voices was a major morale boost for me. They expressed relief that we were safe and had reached the top. I was reminded once again that a high mountain may be tough on a climber, but it is also very tough on wives and kids who must wait, with absolutely no control, no timely information, nor any assurance that you will be coming back.

Bill decided to place a call to his dad in California. Our luck held and he was speaking to Mr. Jackson within minutes. Bill thought his father would get a kick out of a call from Nairobi,

Kenya and he was right. Bill explained our mountaineering success and a few words about the quality of life in Africa. Bill would not be a good spokesperson for the Kenyan or Tanzanian Chambers of Commerce.

While father and son were talking I thought that Mr. Jackson had to be proud of his kid. It isn't every day that your son calls from Africa to tell you that he was thinking of you and loves you. It isn't every kid who travels halfway across the world, drives across African plains, tackles a 19,000 foot snow capped mountain at the equator, and wins.

I guessed that during the cocktail hour a stoic but proud Mr. Jackson would sip a scotch and tell all gathered, "Damnedest thing, my youngest kid called me from Africa. Imagine that. 'Climbed Kilimanjaro just for the hell of it. Big mountain. Tough kid."

It's the kind of thing a father might say to his friends over a drink . . . but might not say to the kid.

Beneath the tough-guy veneer I knew that Bill was a softy and it didn't surprise me a bit when he hung up and then wiped away a few tears. It was a phone call both father and son would not forget. It was a memory that Bill would re-discover a few years later when his father died.

Africa taught many lessons, but this one was special: speak the things you feel to people you care about while they can still hear you.

Give them flowers while they live.

Nairobi, Kenya
Friday, June 12ᵗʰ

Revisiting Nairobi—Would You Like A Slice of Zebra?

Just how many events, discoveries and adventures can you pack into one day? We would test the limits of this question.

There was a knock on the hotel door, a very early knock. I stumbled to the door and opened it just a crack. Behold, a barefoot New Zealand lady, dressed and ready for adventure. Frankie Spite had found us. I quickly threw on some hiking shorts and invited her in.

Frankie, ever soft of voice, asked if she might use our shower. I offered her towels and she enjoyed hot water and finely milled English soap. Refreshed and ready to go, she elected to accompany Bill to the native open market. When David arrived we agreed to visit the Kenyan Brewerie, Ltd. David felt that Tusker t-shirts would make dandy gifts for friends. African beer was almost unknown in the USA and the shirts would be a curiosity.

David navigated and I drove through the chaotic Nairobi traffic. We found the brewery and David's charm and diplomacy soon had us in the office of the marketing director. He was dressed in a neat gray suit with a stripped red tie. He explained their markets and showed us maps to indicate outlets. All pins stopped at the Tanzanian border. I saw the dot for Namanaga and heard the words, "What makes you think you can take that truck out of the country?" The official logic seemed to apply to beer sales as well.

"And have you tried our Tusker lager," asked the marketing director?

"Oh yes," replied David, with a smile. "Patrick here has done quite a study of Tusker, haven't you, mate? It is a good brew, don't you think?"

Maintaining just a little integrity, I nodded and smiled, but said nothing. I thought about an old line from my Wisconsin days. We brewed just a little bit of beer in the Badger State, but some of it was marginal. It was said of one local brew, "This beer is like making love in a canoe . . . very close to water."

I asked the director about the firm's marketing activities. With great enthusiasm he described several promotional programs, including an annual golf tournament. I probed for evidence of marketing activities beyond promotion and got nothing of substance. Like many American businesses the Kenyan Brewerie viewed marketing as merely a promotional scheme, a method of disposing of production. I wondered if they would ever learn that you cannot promote your way to success, if the product does not satisfy the customer. It is a hard lesson and as a consultant with years of marketing experience, I confess that some of my clients have yet to really live the concept, in spite of my coaching and pleading. You can, after all, lead an elephant to water, but you can't force him to drink. Many companies still attempt to sell what they have chosen to make, rather than selling what customers want to buy.

I love to teach and I was tempted to share some of my mistakes, my bloody noses and skinned knees and a few victories with the marketing man. But I was keenly aware that he knew more than I would ever know about his neighborhood. As former Speaker of The House, Tip O'Neil so wisely put it, "All politics is local." The same can be said for marketing.

The marketing director, a gentleman in every way, picked up his phone and called the storehouse. "I'm sending my friends from America to you. Please help them to whatever they require and thank-you for your cooperation."

We shook hands and thanked him most sincerely. He smiled and bowed and we were on our way to the storehouse.

"Nice chap," observed David.

"Oh yes, and he did say 'whatever they require.'"

"Oh yes, mate, that he did."

We waited for the storehouse man to take our order. There were premium and promotional items everywhere, all bearing the Tusker logo, a charging bull elephant. We looked at posters, t-shirts, signs, golf visors, napkins, umbrellas and more. Name it and they had it. It was a premium salesman's dream house. I also noticed four large yellow busses with the logo and the name "Tusker" on the side. The busses were used to transport people during the firm's annual golf tournament and other special promotional events.

The storehouse man approached. "Director, he say, you may have what you like."

David immediately asked for Tusker t-shirts.

In a low secretive voice I said, "David, ask him if we can have a bus."

"In addition to the t-shirts, mate, we would also like a bus."

He returned with an ample supply of t-shirts.

"And the bus?" said Mr. Shrock of the Straight Faced Shrocks.

"Ohhhh, no bus, no bus, busses all gone for long while. Sorry, busses gone." He nodded apologetically and walked away, sincere to the end.

In the afternoon, I suggested to Bill that we try to locate the home of Beryl Markham, a remarkable Englishwoman who was the first female to fly solo across the Atlantic. I had just read her autobiography, *West With The Night* and wished to thank her for writing a marvelous book and for her incredible courage. She would be in her eighties and in your eighties you need to hear good things about your life whenever you can.

I approached the very capable Norfolk Hotel concierge and explained my interest in locating Miss Markham. He listened patiently and with his hands folded in front of him he looked down at the carpet and said, "I am so sorry. You cannot see her. Miss Markham died a few months ago."

I stood there, saddened by the news and feeling as if I had lost a friend. That's what wonderful authors do. They create a bond with the reader. I truly felt as if I'd known her.

Since Bill and I both have extensive hospital management experience we decided to visit the Nairobi Hospital and the Kenyan medical school to compare African healthcare with American healthcare. What we found was not so different from American hospitals I had worked in early in my career. The only real difference was time. The hospital I saw in Nairobi was a hospital I had seen twenty years earlier in America.

I decided to walk the halls and wandered onto a medical in-patient floor. I dodged meal and supply carts as white uniformed nurses and orderlies went about their mid-day chores. Suddenly I was back in time. It was Memorial Hospital, the summer of 1961. I was working as an orderly to help pay for my college education. It was my first hospital job and in many respects it was the best job I ever had. I earned eighty-three cents an hour and the right to provide hands-on care to sick people who were very grateful for the kindness and personal attention I was able to provide. In a small way, I helped them through one of the worst moments of their lives.

Although thousands of miles and several years from my hospital roots, as I watched the familiar ballet of uniformed workers going through their routines, I felt very much at home. How far, yet how near.

There is constant motion in a hospital as hundreds of individual actions mesh to provide non-stop patient care. I moved down the crowded corridors with ease. The hospital was old and a bit worn, but very clean. The African personnel I passed smiled and said polite "hellos." No jamboing in the hospital I noted. It was a friendly atmosphere, a condition often missing in more technically oriented American hospitals. Our hospitals, I lamented, could use an infusion of humanism. Warm and friendly works. Cold and technical is, well, cold and technical. Patients need and expect a high level of technical quality, but they want to be treated as human beings. Empathy is high on their list of wants.

The patient rooms in Nairobi were small and crowded. The beds were the old hand crank models. One was equipped with a wooden trapeze for orthopedic patients. There was an antiseptic smell in the air, and occasionally a whiff of sickness and death. Yet spirits seemed mostly positive. Even family members and patients would frequently nod and smile as I passed.

The more I walked, the more I observed, the more it became 1961 and I was coming on the night shift at Memorial to care for a dozen patients. I could picture the skinny lad dressed in starched whites who didn't look old enough to be taking care of anyone. I remember the smiles from some patients as I popped into a room to greet them and tell them I'd be coming back to take care of them. They were happy to see me, in most cases, and grateful for whatever I could do for them.

I can still see the face of the old farmer who was near death. I would come in and clean him up, tighten his sheets, fluff his pillows, turn him gently, and rub his back with lotion. He would hold my hand for a few minutes. His rough old hand, which had been as strong as a vice, was now weak and cool. He would smile and tell me I reminded him of his grandson. He said the very same thing to me every night. And then one night when I came on duty he was gone. I worked most of the 11:00 PM to 7:00 AM shift with a lump in my throat. He was dead and I had not had the opportunity to say "goodbye." But I was grateful I had given him some care and comfort in the final moments of his life.

The memories were warm and rich.

As I left the African hospital I paused to make a picture of a sign that asked visitors to be " . . . . especially kind to the nurses who have a great deal to do for the patients." It was a nice, practical and very British inspired sign.

As I raised my Nikon to make the picture two physicians appeared and crossed the parking lot toward me. I said "hello" in my best American voice.

"How about a photograph of two native doctors? Shall we pose for you?" They laughed and walked on with no intention of posing for me.

"Yes, that would be very good. But could you each hold a spear?"

They laughed with less conviction and moved along to make their rounds.

We moved on to the entrance of the Kenyatta Medical School complex. At a distance the hospital is a modern looking structure, one of the most modern looking buildings in Nairobi, or perhaps all of Kenya. As we got closer we noticed that patient rooms opened onto balconies, much like an American motel. Patient clothing and bed linens were draped over the railings outside the patient rooms, airing in the afternoon sun . . . . and dust.

Bill wanted one last shot at the native market in central Nairobi. He felt he could swap his running shoes for goods. He wanted a piece of African jewelry for his wife-to-be and the shoes were valuable.

Personally, I wanted to see him in action. It would be a contest. The sandy haired, white, Irish-American, Nebraska trained, ex-jock versus the black, street-wise Kenyan traders. It would be the American, with limited trading experience, versus the African traders with deep professional experience.

The market is a single square block of mud and open stalls. The staples are carved wooden animals, woven purses and jewelry. Everything is for sale, including goods you cannot see.

We wandered through the milling crowd passing one hawker after another. Everyone proclaimed the best, the cheapest. After a few minutes it was clear we were the only white faces in the square. But the natives were friendly and we returned their greetings and "jamboed" our way around the market square.

Bill found the jewelry he wanted and began his pitch. The seller was a middle-aged Kenyan dressed in blue jeans and wearing ragged looking shoes. They were scuffed and nicked and had not seen any polish in their lifetime.

Bill offered his running shoes, which he had cleaned up in the bathtub at the Norfolk Hotel. They looked pretty good.

"Shoes not enough," said the Kenyan, who tried to look disinterested, a classic bartering technique. "Shoes and money."

"No, bad deal. Shoes only," replied the American trader. "Shoes for jewelry."

The native held his position, but it now became shoes and less money.

"No deal, shoes only," said a determined Jackson.

I don't know if it was deliberate or just a tactical error, but the Kenyan hung his head, feigned displeasure, but was definitely able to see his battered shoes. He looked up at Bill. The clean running shoes were hanging around Bill's neck, resting on his chest.

Bill took the shoes off his chest and handed them toward the native. "Here, take them, try them on, see if they fit, see if you like them." The Kenyan stepped back. Bill advanced. The Kenyan, feigning reluctance, took the shoes with no expression.

Sotto voice to me, Bill said, "If he puts them on it's over."

Bill picked up the jewelry, the native held the shoes. No money was on the table.

"Try 'em, go ahead, put them on. Great shoes."

"Shoes and money," repeated the Kenyan. And he bent over and began putting on the shoes. Once they were on, he shuffled to test the fit. No expression.

"Shoes and money," the Kenyan said, now with a slight smile on his face.

"No deal. Take 'em off, mate. We're outta here. No deal. We're gone. Safari sana."

"Shoes not enough, need money," repeated the native, now with less conviction.

"Even up, jewelry for shoes, or you take off the shoes."

Bill advanced toward the Kenyan motioning for him to give the shoes back. The native moved back and walked from side to side in his stall.

He finally turned, flashed a big self-conscious smile, and waved us off.

It was over. The deal was done. Shoes for jewelry and no money changed hands. As we walked away I wondered just who had actually come out on top. It was Bill's $70 running shoes versus some native crafted jewelry. Given the economics of a third world country, I had the feeling that we had made one native very happy indeed.

The Carnivore

David Schrock had promised a "unique" dining experience in Nairobi. The word unique is troublesome. Well, perhaps the users of the word unique are troublesome. Very little in the whole wide world is truly unique. But, in this case David was entirely accurate.

David and Frankie met us in the Lord Dellemere pub at the Norfolk. We drove north on dark rural roads in search of a restaurant called The Carnivore.

Imagine a restaurant built around a circular fire pit, perhaps fifteen feet in diameter. Imagine a dozen iron racks inside the perimeter of the fire pit, capable of holding large rods or skewers of meat. Imagine native "carvers" in long aprons adjusting the skewers or spits up and down, turning them to position the meat either closer to the fire or further from the fire. Envision their shiny black faces, covered with perspiration, glistening in the reflected light of the dancing flames. Watch them as they constantly baste large chunks of meat with brushes as big as six inch house painting brushes, coating every conceivable form of African game with oil and herbs.

Dante's Inferno had come to life.

We were seated at a table not far from the fire pit and all the roasting action. David, smiling broadly, turned to me and said, "What do you think of the Carnivore, mate?"

"Mr. Shrock, were I a vegetarian, this would be the very definition of hell. Since I'm not a vegetarian, this is heaven on a very hot tropical day."

David laughed harder than I had ever seen him laugh. I thought my response was humorous, but certainly not *that* funny.

Now, attempting to suppress his laughter, David grasped my arm and said, "Patrick . . . (laughter) . . . you see . . . (laughter) . . . . Frankie . . . (laughter) . . . . IS a vegetarian."

I looked at Frankie and she just nodded her head and produced a very slight smile as if to say, "So, there."

Except for Frankie Spite, we were the carnivores. Large white plates appeared. Pitchers of cold beer appeared and the consumption of roasted beast was underway.

Meat carvers circulated throughout the meal each carrying a different type of roasted meat, direct from the fire pit, sizzling and dripping all the way. By the end of the meal the floors were more than a little slick. As were the plates.

The gloved handed carvers would approach our table, holding the skewer or spit vertically and inquire as to your needs. For example, they would simply say, "Zebra?"

It wasn't exactly a question for they were going to slice some Zebra whether you wanted it or not. The carver would stand the spit next to your plate, angle the lump of meat over your plate and inquire about your taste. "How?" This was a question. If you said medium rare he would rotate the spit to the side of the roast that was approximately medium rare. Out would come a very big and very sharp butcher knife and, before your very nose and close to your ear, the knife would come down on the meat and a healthy portion of roasted beast would drop to your plate. Most of the time. If the meat missed your plate the waiter would merely spear it with the tip of the knife, sometimes embedding the knife in the wooden table top, and flip the errant meat onto your plate without so much as a "Sorry about that, old chap."

"You want Zebra?"

A skeptical Bill replied, "Well, yeah, I guess I'll take some zebra."

"How?"

Bill adjusted his glasses, something he does to buy time. "I've never had zebra, so how do you do it best? I don't know?"

The waiter glared at him. The meat dripped. Bill adjusted his glasses again.

"Medium, I guess. Yeah, medium."

The waiter rotated the spit, the large knife moved through the air within inches of Bill's head. Faster than you could say "I think I'll have a grilled cheese and a cup of tomato soup instead" two generous pieces of zebra hit the plate. It was red. Bill adjusted his glasses six or seven times.

I was next. Let's see, zebra is actually a horse. Hmmm. I had no glasses to adjust so I invoked the Mages Law on food—try everything, except brocolli and brussle sprouts, at least once, never eat anything that is still moving, and don't eat anything bigger than your head.

"Yes, zebra please."

"How?"

"Medium rare, please."

He leaned the spit over my plate. Something dripped on my leg. The knife passed my face by a few inches and I could see that it was sharp. There were many fine little nicks on the blade. He rotated the spit and in a flash two medium rare pieces of red meat hit my plate with a splat. It was a truly interesting sound. Something you would hear in a coyote-roadrunner cartoon.

David merely motioned to the carver and three generous pieces hit his plate. David smiled broadly.

I cut into the zebra cautiously. This was an entirely new experience. Roasted zebra had the texture of prime rib. It was delicious and slightly sweet. Bill, equally cautious, shrugged and cut a second piece. In the meantime, David had inhaled his zebra and was looking for more.

Frankie received a beautiful plate of assorted grilled and steamed vegetables. The presentation was worthy of a fine dining establishment. She was more than pleased and I gave Carnivore management a great deal of credit for understanding the customer. Here, in the Super Bowl of roasted meat, appeared a grand garden of plants.

I looked at Frankie, and in my best imitation of our Kilimanjaro guide, Felix The Comedian, I said, "Animals eat plants, you eat animals, you get plants." She smiled, and in the dancing firelight of The Carnivore the New Zealand lady looked absolutely beautiful.

Carvers circulated with spits of dripping roasts. The aroma of fat in the fire was almost intoxicating. Conversation was limited. Meat was consumed in great quantity.

We sampled zebra, wildebeest, antelope, warthog, water buffalo, chicken, beef and several chunks of mystery meat. I lost track after eight portions.

The antelope was outstanding. It was the best venison I have ever tasted. All voted antelope number one and we decided that roast antelope would probably put antelope on the endangered species list. Zebra came in a close second—Africa's prime rib.

The rest of the beasts came under the heading of "noble experiment." I can promise you there will be no McWildebeest on MacDonald's menu. Warthog will not appear in trendy New York restaurants. Water buffalo do make for good wallets. Argentina and Iowa need not fear competition from African beef. Message to Frank Perdue—your chickens are extraordinary.

Bill and I tried everything, but did not finish everything. But David certainly did. At one point I cut a small piece off a large slab of African hog and had great difficulty getting it down. When David heard my displeasure and refusal to consume the rest of the pork, his fork quickly hit my plate and I found out that pigs can fly.

David lobbied the passing carvers for more antelope, more antelope, how about some more antelope? The request seemed to fall on deaf ears. I got up, went to the fire pit and located a roasting chunk of antelope. I discovered that the fire pit area was damned hot and developed instant respect for the carvers who worked the pit and basted the meat. I asked a carver if we might have some antelope so he lifted the hot spit, brought it to our table and carved away. Delicious. During the rest of the meal, however, our pleas for antelope went unfulfilled. The carvers knew, no doubt, that they must dispense the other lesser cuts.

When we finally drained our fourth or fifth pitcher of beer and pushed back from the table, stuffed and sated, we agreed that the meal was one of the most unusual dinning experiences we had ever had and another bite of anything was impossible. Frankie scolded us playfully for putting a dent in the wildlife of Africa, praised her vegetables and disclosed that we had resembled a pack of wild dogs in a feeding frenzy.

We laughed and agreed.

A carver stopped at our table and said, "Antelope?" We painfully declined, stuffed as we were.

I lifted my beer glass and toasted the group.

Then another carver stopped at our table with a dripping spit of meat. "Antelope?" he said with a wicked smile.

The preferred antelope was now safe from the American carnivores, and the carvers knew it.

Following the beast feast, we drove Frankie and David to the airport for their midnight flight to London. David provided directions while I negotiated the dark roads on the outskirts of Nairobi. It was my day to drive.

"Fuel check, big guy," said an ever-alert William Jackson.

I checked the fuel gage and we were in need. "Better get some," I said.

"On the left, there's an Aggipe station. Swing around and let's fill her up," said Jackson.

"No good, mate," advised David Shrock.

"What do you mean, no good?" said Bill.

"Aggipe is gas-oil, mate."

"Gas-oil? You mean like diesel fuel?"

"That's it lad, it's like diesel fuel. No good for this truck. You need gas, regular petrol."

Silence.

Even in the dark of the truck I could tell Jackson was turning red and about to pop.

"No, ohhhhhh noooooooooooooooo. I put Aggipe in the truck when I filled up at the Nogorongoro Crater."

And there it was. No wonder the truck didn't work well going into the crater and down the road to Arusha. No wonder we had distributed large clouds of black smoke all the way from Ngorongoro to Arusha. And no wonder things improved greatly when I filled the truck with petrol before the drive from Arusha to Nairobi. Jackson had loaded us with gas-oil.

Airport goodbyes are not my favorite event. I had grown very fond of David and Frankie. And we had suffered the challenge of climbing one of the world's incredible mountains. We had a wonderful bond and something told me I would not see them again. We hugged, promised to write and exchanged misty-eyed farewell waves as they headed for the British Air gate. It was a sad moment. It always is when you leave someone you respect and truly care about.

Nairobi, Kenya
Saturday, June 13th

Can You Carry A Masai Spear Onto A Boeing 747?

At the airport we checked in, holding our carry-on in one hand and our six foot Masai hunting spears in the other. Kenyan British Air ticket agents saw nothing unusual. Spears are common tools in Africa.

Then we advanced to customs. Once again native agents stamped our passports and sent us through. Two white guys in bush dress carrying spears? No problem.

We approached a military checkpoint. Two uniformed native guards with assault rifles looked us over, provided the standard issue sullen glare and passed us through. Spears? No problem.

And then we approached the podium at the jet way and met the white British purser. He looked resplendent in a well-tailored navy blue suit, white shirt and rep tie—a true professional, everything including the stiff upper lip. He looked us over verrrry carefully. Spears? Big problem.

"Where do you think you are going with that spear, sir?"

I smiled and mustered as much boyish charm as possible. "Why, to London, of course, to visit the Queen."

He folded his arms across his chest and drilled me in the eyes. "Not on my 747 you are not."

Silence. He was waiting for an explanation and was not very happy with us.

"Isn't there a safe place we could store the spears in flight, I would hate to check them."

"Absolutely not, out of the question. The spears must be checked. They must go in the hold."

"I really prize this spear and would hate to lose it or have it damaged." I actually whined a little.

He spoke in slow deliberate cadence. "Sir, the spear is a dangerous weapon and we simply cannot have dangerous weapons in the cabin of the aircraft. It is out of the question, really!"

Jackson, standing behind me, protested. "That is a bad deal."

"No spears in the cabin and that IS the final word."

Jackson again. "That's ridiculous, who ever heard of hijacking a 747 with a Masai spear?"

Stop the music!

There's the magic word. You never, never, ever say "hijack" to an airline person. It is over, I thought. We are now on our way to an African jail.

I looked at Bill and rolled my eyes. He looked astonished, as if he suddenly realized what he had said.

After a tense moment of silence, kind of like that moment when you are resting your neck on a wooden block and waiting for the guillotine blade to drop, the purser turned and walked away. Bill and I waited in silence, holding our lion killing spears and waiting for the big French blade.

Soon a native officer appeared and he motioned for us to step aside and follow him. We complied like the sheep we were. I had visions of interrogation. I had visions of a cell in an African jail. I had visions of being in Africa for a long time. We were directed to two chairs and an empty table. We sat in silence.

I wanted to shout, "NEVER say HIJACK in an AIRPORT!" I couldn't find the energy or the breath.

The officer reappeared carrying newspapers and a roll of masking tape. He motioned for us to place the spears on the table. He proceeded to wrap the spears in paper and tape them securely. He then affixed baggage tags, gave us the stubs and pointed toward the podium and the jetway. All this without a glance at us or a single word. The spears disappeared, presumably to the cavernous hold of the 747. I was so relieved I didn't protest.

The purser never looked at us, simply took our boarding passes and permitted us, allowed us, granted us the privilege of entering Mr. Boeing's wonderful aircraft. Perhaps he had a sense of humor after all. But the fact remains, you simply do not say "hijack" in an airport, even in jest.

It is both interesting and instructive to note that Bill and I both sat in our seats, seat belts connected and watched the open door of the aircraft for any sign of uniforms other than British Air.

The aircraft doors were finally closed, the jet way disconnected and, following a short taxi, the 747 rolled, rotated, began to fly and we were on our way to London. The sound of the massive wheel carriages retracting and the thump of the wheel well doors closing tightly was like a punctuation mark . . . . end of sentence, end of story.

But the story never actually ends when you are traveling. The next paragraph, the next chapter is always there if you are awake and observant.

Life can be an amazing collection of contrasts. As the 747 eased into the sky I noted that we were sitting in air conditioned comfort in one of man's most incredible inventions, a computer driven, jet propelled monster aircraft, capable of at least 550 knots. The population of many of the African villages we had driven through, at a max speed of thirty miles per hour, could be seated in this carpeted cabin with room for the goats and cattle. The airplane was crafted from some of the most sophisticated metals in the world. Yet, nestled somewhere in the belly of this high tech beast were two spears, fashioned from iron and wood, the simplest and most ancient of weapons, forged no doubt, by hand using iron-age designs and methods.

At cruising altitude I requested and received two glasses of Mumm champagne. Bill and I toasted a successful African adventure.

Our flight path took us north over the Kikuyu Hills of Kenya, over the Sudan and over the Sudd, one of the most formidable places on the planet.

I thought once again of Beryl Markham. She had grown up in Kenya and learned to fly at an early age. In 1933 she became the first woman in Africa to receive a pilot's license. She had actually flown from Kenya to England in a single engine aircraft, making frequent stops along the way for fuel and food. In her remarkable book, "*West With The Night*" she expressed her concern about flying over the Sudd in a monoplane. Over the treacherous swamps of the Sudd there was no room for error and no place to land should engine trouble occur. There was also no chance of rescue.

"If you can visualize twelve thousand square miles of swamp" wrote the aviatrix, "that seethes and crawls like a prehistoric crucible of half-formed life, you have a conception of the Sudd."

She characterized the area as "sinister," "treacherous," and "eerie." The stench, she reported, was very strong at one thousand feet.

Beryl Markham flew over the Sudd on one engine. We had four. She had incredible courage.

Later in the flight the first officer was making his rounds, checking out aircraft systems and talking with passengers. I asked him if he knew of Beryl Markham and her flight across the Sudd to England. He had not, so I described her feat and he listened with great interest, noting the title of her book for future reference.

His conclusion, "Gutsy lady, that Markham. Gutsy or crazy. But then she made it, didn't she." He shook my hand and returned to the starship quality of the Boeing cockpit, a palace of triple redundant computerized bells and whistles, all without a single whiff of rotting swamp.

"Marvelous Adventure, I'd Say—Never Met A Bloke Who Climbed Kilimanjaro"

The pounding our bodies and minds had taken on Kilimanjaro and over the rutted trails that passed for roads was becoming a memory. Blisters on feet were healing, bumps, bruises and minor lacerations were fading and aching muscles were beginning to relax. The final challenge was crossing many time zones. Using my long established formula, one day of recovery for every time zone crossed, I figured I might make a complete recovery in time for the next Christmas.

At Heathrow just outside London we made our way to baggage claim. Our equipment packs showed up on time. The spears did not.

We described the packages and the contents. British Air agents were very accommodating and called their baggage handlers. The report was negative, no long newspaper wrapped packages were in evidence.

I implored the agents that they were not looking for "packages" in the normal sense. These were very thin spears, six feet long, etc., etc. They called baggage claim again. Everything, they were told, was off the airplane.

"Gentlemen, please, these spears mean a great deal to us, let me go back there and search myself. Perhaps the spears are in some recessed part of the floor of the hold, they could easily slip under something."

The senior agent gave it a thought and then said, "Tell you what, I'll go back and look for them myself."

Fifteen minutes later the senior agent returned with a big smile on his face. He was carrying two spears. They had indeed been under something. The paper wrapping was tattered, iron blades exposed, but they were in tact. We offered appropriate thanks and apologies for our steam. The agents simply smiled and indicated it was "nothing, really."

The saga of the Masai spears was not over. At customs a kindly British agent said, "Now, what have we here?" I had unwrapped my spear and the four edged blade was now exposed. He reached for the spear before I could speak a warning. He winced and drew back his hand. He was bleeding. He had grasped the iron blade and underestimated the cutting edge. A colleague quickly found some clean cloth and together we wrapped his hand. I wondered what the charge was going to be? Assaulting a Royal Customs Official?

He took a deep breath, looked at my passport, stamped it and said, "Terribly sorry about that, sir. Clumsy of me. Good day and have a pleasant stay in England."

Talk about stiff upper lip and all that.

Sunday morning was misty, gray and cold. I decided to take a walk around historic Grosvenor Square and couldn't resist a few choruses of a Mel Torme inspired, "Foggy Day In London Town."

> "How long I wonder,
> Could this thing possibly last,
> But the age of miracles,
> It had not passed . . . . "

As I walked the Square, waiting for Bill to emerge from the Marriott Hotel, I felt the inner calm one often feels after a particularly strenuous but successful contest. It's a good tired spent feeling and hard to accurately describe.

There was no one in the Square, save the statues of Franklin Roosevelt and General Dwight Eisenhower, no one to hear my singing. FDR and Ike didn't seem to mind and the pigeons seemed to like it, but I reminded myself to always keep my day job.

Bill had an early TWA flight from Heathrow and a killer schedule which took him to New York, St. Louis and finally to Albuquerque. I had a mid-day flight from Gatwick on Delta to Atlanta with an easy connection to Memphis.

I walked Bill to the Underground station. He purchased a ticket, picked up his gear and turned to leave. The adventure was over.

"This is it. See you, big guy."

"Travel safely, William and keep your feet up going over the pond."

The moment deserved something more than "see you around" but I couldn't come up with anything with any class or substance. I hate goodbyes.

We had persisted and endured. It was a tough but rewarding trip, one that could have gone very wrong at many moments. But we had come through intact, wiser and more confident than ever. The days ahead would allow us to sort things out and re-live the moments worth collecting and remembering. It was time to let language rest.

Bill passed through the turnstile and disappeared into the subway system. In addition to his gear he was carrying a Masai spear and a four-foot wooden giraffe. I wondered how many times he would have to explain his possessions between London and New Mexico.

A few hours later I checked out of the hotel and loaded my gear into a classic black London taxi. The driver was a gray-haired grandfather who had been driving the streets of London for a lifetime. He was short and round and wore a black suit and flat gray wool cap. In spite of very thick glasses and failing eyes he threaded the cab through London traffic with a deft touch.

"And where are you headed, sir?"

"I'm on my way home. I live in the States, in Tennessee."

"Tennessee is it? And you've been on holiday, have you?"

I must have looked rather curious. Beneath an African bush hat with one side of the brim snapped to the crown, I sported a two week growth of stubble. It did not quite qualify as a beard. I was wearing a khaki bush shirt with epaulets, twill pants, ragg wool socks and very weathered mountain boots. And I held a Masai hunting spear in my right hand. I was not your average fare.

"Yes, sir, I've been to Africa."

"Why that's bloody marvelous. Africa, you say?"

"Kenya and Tanzania."

"Bloody marvelous. Were there animals about?"

I described lots of animals and he was duly impressed. We pulled up at Victoria Station where I would catch a train to Gatwick Airport.

"That was it then, a trip to Africa to see the animals?"

"Yes, and also to climb a mountain, Mt. Kilimanjaro, the highest mountain on the African Continent." I climbed out of the cab. He opened his door and followed. He looked at me with a combination of awe and curiosity. His eyes were very large.

"You went to climb Kili-man-jar-oh?" He pronounced every syllable as if they were separate names.

"Yes, we reached the summit after a four day climb." I pulled my gear out of the cab and he hurried around to help.

"Why I've never met anyone who's climbed a mountain. You climbed Kili-man-jar-o? Bless you now. And you did it, did you?"

"Yes, but it is done quite a bit these days, many people climb it. It's a tough trek, but I'll be you could do it." I was chiding him and he knew it.

"Nonsense, bloody nonsense it is. The likes of me couldn't be going up a mountain now. In me prime maybe, but I'm too old in the tooth today. Have trouble getting into bed, I do."

"I'll bet that's not what your wife says."

He laughed and slapped my arm. "She does say I'm still fit and strong as a barge pole." He roared with laughter and I roared with him.

"You're off to America then. And you did it. Never met a bloke who climbed Kili-man-jar-oh." He looked around at the passing faces on the street as if he were sharing something special.

"Bloody marvelous old man. Bless you now, I've something to tell the grandchildren tonight."

"Tell them their grandfather is the best taxi driver in London and please quote me." He beamed.

"Ah, but you, you did it. The highest, you say. Quite a journey you've had, all the way to the top of Africa."

"Yes, and for a few minutes we may have been the highest people on the planet."

"Imagine that. Bloody marvelous." The smile covered his entire face.

I paid him and he took my hand in both of his. "Be taking care of yourself and have a safe trip. I'll tell them about you tonight."

As I turned to go he gave me a fatherly pat on the shoulder. He was having such a great time I hated to leave.

I looked back when I reached the door to the station. He was still standing there smiling and waving.

The remaining seat on the train to Gatwick was a double section that faced another empty seat. I stashed my equipment bag and held my spear upright between my knees with one hand on the wooden shaft which connected the killing blade at the top with the pointed iron cattle prod at the bottom. People filed onto the train, but no one took the seat directly across from me. Some preferred to stand rather than sit next to the man with the scruffy beard, wearing bush kit, and holding a spear.

Just before the train began to move a petite English grandmum arrived and seated herself directly across from me. She wore a pill box hat with a veil, spotless white gloves and a rose print dress. She held her black purse on her knees, clasped her hands on the purse, placed her feet and knees together and looked me over from head to toe.

If Norman Rockwell would have been on board he would have been sketching like crazy. The contrast was incredible.

I took some solace in the fact that, while I looked rough, I was clean. My clothes were wrinkled but clean and my manners were in tact.

"Good morning, mam," I said, with a reassuring smile.

She took a visible deep breath, sat up straight, pursed her lips and never took her eye off my spear . . . . all the way to Gatwick. When the train stopped she vanished like a flash of lightening. Not even so much as a "goodbye."

"You can't be carrying that spear on board the aircraft."

Here we go again, I thought, as a Delta agent checked my spear and sent it to the hold of the plane with the rest of the luggage.

"I don't want to lose it."

"No problem, we will give it special handling. Just pick it up in baggage claim in Atlanta, pass through customs and check it to Memphis." Eight hours later I was greatly relieved when a Delta agent in Atlanta brought my spear to luggage pick up. "Here you go, sir, welcome home."

Later that day I was sitting in my kitchen with a glass of Mumm champagne in hand, sharing my trip with a small welcoming committee. At one point I looked out the window

and my son, Matt, then twelve years old, was leading a procession of the little guys of the
neighborhood. They were carrying a variety of sticks and broom handles. He was carrying an
African spear.

Epilogue

Since climbing Mt. Kilimanjaro I have climbed mountains or attempted to climb mountains on five of the seven continents and traveled to six. The adventures have produced wonder and joy and a significant measure of personal growth.

I have learned several lessons from travels to many corners of the world, however one lesson emerges as the greatest and the best. No matter where you set foot, whether it is a small rural village in southern Russia, a stone hut in Nepal, a simple lean-to in the jungles of Tanzania, on the great sand of the Sahara, or passing through a lock on the River Thames in England you meet wonderful people, people who share the same needs and wants, the same hopes and dreams, the same joys and fears. You learn that for all their apparent differences, people the world over are really not that different. You learn the fundamental meaning of life is that we are all on this planet to take care of one another. And when you reach out to provide that care, most often someone reaches back.

Although two heart attacks and subsequent operations have ended my high altitude mountaineering days, I've found many new adventures putting a canoe in the water in unusual places. I've paddled a native canoe through the Panama Canal, paddled my Mad River Lamoille canoe the circumference of Manhattan Island, and have worked my way down the upper Mississippi River in northern Minnesota. I recently concluded paddling the length of the historic River Thames in England, from the source in the Cotswold's, through London and on to Greenwich, home of the international dateline. For over 15 years I have also participated in the Memphis In May Mississippi River Canoe Race, sponsored by the wonderful crew at Outdoors, a shop that has kept me supplied with paddles, life jackets, canoe and myriad other necessities of life.

My friends and fellow canoe adventurers Professor Extraordinaire, Jim Carman, Kensington, California; Louis Knox White, El Dorado, Arkansas; Bill Jackson, Albuquerque, New Mexico; Professor Phil Kolbe, Memphis, Tennessee and my son, Matthew Mages have aided and abetted this process and I'm honored to have traveled in a canoe with them.

One of my personal writing goals is to make the point that one does not have to be super-human or a gifted athlete to take on an adventure and enjoy it. Ordinary people like you and me can accomplish extra-ordinary things if we are willing to prepare, to stretch and reach, take a few risks and smell the flowers along the way.

I strongly suggest, as you travel, take plenty of notes so you can bring back the stories. Always bring back the stories and share the wealth of your experience. Friends and acquaintances will be richer for it. They will be able to see and imagine a slice of life they may never personally experience. The stories, shared freely with others, are a wonderful gift.

The satisfaction of writing a book like *Journey To The Top Of Africa,* however flawed and perhaps even tedious at times, is greatly surpassed by the satisfaction of sharing the story with people who may never travel to East Africa, much less climb to the white roof of Africa, more than three and a half miles into the sky.

William C. Jackson

The part of "Bill Jackson," was played by William C. Jackson of Albuquerque, New Mexico, my long-time friend. He is not responsible for my description or interpretation of his actions or his quotes. Bill's strength on the trail in Africa often motivated me to continue on. For that, for his super-active brain, his sometimes outrageous sense of humor, his great taste in all good things (he is a Green Bay Packer fan) and his friendship, I'm entirely grateful.

Goodluck Christopher

Without Tanzanian native and first rate Kilimanjaro guide, Goodluck Christopher I would not have made the summit. His quiet patience, empathy and persistence got us both to the top of Africa. When we made the summit photo I insisted he stand with me. Wherever you are Goodluck, may the Gods of Kilimanjaro keep you safe.

Robert Kraus, MD

More than twenty years of mountain climbing and high adventure have also produced one episode of pulmonary edema and two heart attacks resulting in two heart operations. It is a testimony to the great skill and medical judgment of my friend and personal physician, Dr. Robert Kraus, Memphis, Tennessee, that I'm still drawing breath and constantly on the go. Dr. Kraus examines and treats the entire patient, and doesn't simply respond to the physical symptoms. He has phenomenal insight and usually has the answer before I have the question. But the quality I appreciate the most is his ability to teach. Dr. Robert is a wonderful teacher and his careful reasoning, his descriptions, explanations, and treatment decisions have given me the confidence to continue to stretch and reach and grow in spite of advanced coronary artery disease. No matter how troubled or down I am, after every visit with Dr. Kraus and his wonderful assistant Debbie, I leave feeling I can handle any challenge life provides. I've worked with thousands of physicians in my career and I'm of the opinion there are MD's and there are RD's. Dr. Robert is an RD, a Real Doctor. He claims my adventures have taught his family geography.

Matthew Michael Mages

My son, Matt Mages was responsible for this book in more ways than he knows. I drafted the book when he was sixteen, thinking I would leave something tangible behind for him. I never really knew my grandfathers and I thought a book on my experience on Kilimanjaro would be something he could read to his children one day. They would then know something of their grandfather Pat, and have some additional insights into their father, Matthew M.

I didn't like the first draft of the book, so I put it on the shelf for many years. Unfinished business has a way or rearing its ugly head. It did, several times, so I decided to re-write the book in 2004. Matt is now thirty and a genuine computer guru. He convinced me the book could be published, should be published and then led the charge to master the new computer technology, help with the design and graphics and literally see the book through production. What began as something I wanted to give to him has become something he has, in part, given me.

We both hope this is the first of many book projects.

Professor James M. "Jim" Carman

I put the finishing touches on this manuscript with a heavy heart and the deepest sadness I have ever experienced. My great friend and my mentor, Jim Carman died on December 9, 2004. In the final hours I flew from Memphis to San Francisco but was unable to reach his bedside in time to say good-bye. His wonderful family, wife and best friend Carol Carman, son Paul and daughters Barbara and Kathy were with him at the end, touching him, holding him, telling Jim stories and helping him through the final moments.

Jim is the finest man I have ever known.

I hate to speak about Jim in the past tense for that is admitting I won't see him again, a supremely painful thought. It makes me want to pull the covers over my head and hide from the reality of it all.

Jim was a professor in the prestigious Haas Graduate School of Business at the University of California at Berkeley. At one point he served as Dean, but he preferred teaching to administration. He achieved professor emeritus status and was loved and respected by one and all.

Professor Carman was internationally known in his field and served, by invitation, as visiting faculty in Ireland, England, France, Norway, Australia and several other countries. He also advised foreign governments on trade issues, served on a hospital board of trustees and consulted with organizations far and wide. But these achievements do not begin to explain the man.

He was purely the most intelligent human being I've ever met. He was also kind, humble, patient and empathetic. Sadly enough these qualities do not often come together in one person, particularly in those with advanced degrees who often seem to believe they really are smarter and better than the rest of us.

Jim was simply Jim. Some of us search for a lifetime to determine who we are. Jim knew who he was. No pretense. His positive attitude and his demeanor caused people to seek him out and open up to him. His encouragement and support encouraged people to strive and seek and grow.

He had a marvelous sense of humor and could easily laugh at himself. He not only knew many things, but Jim also understood so many things that one could talk with him endlessly about any topic. The ancient Greek with the lantern searching for an honest man could have concluded his search with Jim Carman. As the Chinese would say, "He was alive." A high compliment. After words like brilliant and phenomenal my vocabulary fails me.

Jim's special academic interest was marketing, attempting to understand why people make the choices they make. He would then translate his analysis into practical applied and hope that organizations would make better and more satisfying connections with the people they purport to serve. In the parlance of the marketing world, Dr. Carman's product and his service offering can be described as *the human spirit*—he absolutely glowed with it. If his product was a brand, then the brand was simply "Jim."

Listening was one of Jim's very special qualities. He listened so well I think he actually invented listening. I recall once, in our many travels to far away places, Jim and I were seated with a lady who wanted to talk. Jim was intent on reading but he graciously set his reading aside and listened to her. At one point she paused long enough to ask him what he did in life. The illustrious professor said in a soft, low key voice, "I'm a teacher."

At the time I thought his answer was the very definition of understatement.

As my friend Bill Gjetson, said so beautifully, "Jim had the skill and the heart and the courage to teach, for students can be very harsh critics." There are, no doubt, students all over the world who loved Jim Carman.

It was my great, good fortune to hike with Jim, climb mountains, paddle a canoe, and explore foreign lands with him. But the best times with Jim were the long and thoughtful conversations. How I cherished those moments.

This book, my first, is dedicated to him. It was an easy decision since he inspired me for over thirty years and often coached me up and over many of life's great mountains, attempting in his classy way to teach me, to encourage me to find understanding and the greater meaning, to make me better. Through it all I maintained one clear and very lofty goal—I wanted to be like Jim.

Jim didn't climb Kilimanjaro with us, although I wish he had. I was 45 years old at the time and I struggled to get to the summit. Jim was a few years older and certainly could have done it, but he waited to climb Kilimanjaro until he was in his prime . . . . at age 73. And he didn't struggle.

What an amazing man.

I am happy you chose to read *Journey To The Top Of Africa*. I'm glad you decided to take this trip with me and I hope we can travel together again soon.

Patrick Mages, Germantown, Tennessee, USA   July 4, 2005

Contact the author via E-Mail: *patrick@journeytothetopofafrica.com*
Also visit the website!: *www.journeytothetopofafrica.com*

Book Notes

Cover Illustration
The cover illustration is a 16x20 painting, acrylic on canvas and was designed and painted by the author.

Pen & Ink Illustration
The pen and ink drawings and maps were designed and drawn by the author.

Author Photo
Jane Malton photographed the author in his canoe on Spring Lake, Mississippi.

Book Production & General Encouragement
Matthew M. Mages

Contact the Author:
E-Mail: *patrick@journeytothetopofafrica.com*
WWW: *www.journeytothetopofafrica.com*

Postal Mail: P.O. Box 381453
              Germantown, TN
              38183 USA

Contact the Publisher:
E-Mail: *info@saintbrendanpress.com*
WWW: *www.saintbrendanpress.com*

Resources

The following books and publications were very useful and provided facts and insight about Mt. Kilimanjaro, the Ngorongoro Crater and life in East Africa.

Kilimanjaro: The White Roof Of Africa
Harold Lange
Edition Leipzig, GDR, 1982

West With The Night
Beryl Markham
North Point Press, Sausalito, California, USA, 1983

(Beryl Markham grew up in East Africa and was the first pilot to fly solo across the Atlantic from England to North America. Lindberg was the first to fly west to east in 1927. Markham flew east to west in 1936. The book describes her life in East Africa and the Atlantic flight.)

Different Drums: A Doctor's Forty Years In East Africa
Dr. Michael Wood
Century Hutchinson Ltd., Covent Garden, London, UK, 1987

(Dr. Wood was co-founder of Kenya's Flying Doctor Service. He was Knighted in 1985 for his service to humanity.)

Seven Summits

Bass, Wells, Ridgeway

Warner Books, New York, USA, 1986

(Dick Bass was the first to climb the highest mountain on each of the seven continents.)

Backpacker's Africa: A Walker's Guide to East, Central and Southern Africa

Hillary Bradt

Bradt Enterprises, Bucks, England, 1983

Mountain Names

Robert Hixson Julyan

The Mountaineers, Seattle, Washington, USA, 1984

National Geographic

The National Geographic Society

Washington, DC, USA

(*National Geographic* is an international treasure. Many useful articles were available in back issues on Mt. Kilimanjaro, the Ngorongoro Crater and East Africa.)